JANE PACKER
Living with flowers

JANE PACKER

Living with flowers

Photography by Simon Brown

Text in association with Jane Martin

Trafalgar Square Publishing

For my family, Gary,
Rebby, and Lola xxx.

First published in the United States of America
in 1997 by
Trafalgar Square Publishing
North Pomfret
Vermont 05053

First published in Great Britain in 1997 by
Conran Octopus Limited
37 Shelton Street
London WC2H 9HN

Printed in Hong Kong

ISBN 1 57076 079 9

Library of Congress Catalog Card Number: 96-61471

Senior Editor: Jenna Jarman
Editorial Assistant: Helen Woodhall
Copy Editor: Catherine Ward

Art Director: Helen Lewis
Art Editor: Leslie Harrington
Stylist: Cathy Sinker

Production: Julia Golding

Index: Indexing Specialists

Right (clockwise from top left):
'First Red' rose , echinops, ranunculus, primrose
Overleaf: Euphorbia, ranunculus and peonies with pink
'Prophyra' roses and orange 'Lambada' roses

CONTENTS

CITY 8   **Stylish and contemporary**
With attitude

COUNTRY 54   **Fresh and natural**
For informal interiors

SEA 98   **Cool and serene**
Utter simplicity

GARDEN 120   **Easy and relaxed**
Outdoor living

FOREWORD

The world of flowers has been revolutionized in the twenty-something years since my first experience of the flower industry – a Saturday job I had in a local florist's shop. Flowers are much more affordable now, and more widely available, not only from florists but from street vendors, supermarkets, and even gas stations. The result is that many people now buy flowers on a regular basis, for every day as well as for special occasions. And this is what LIVING WITH FLOWERS, *my most personal book to date, is all about.*

For a long time now, I have wanted to write a book that treats flowers simply and naturally – no tricks, no complicated displays, just arrangements that would appeal to people who are short of time but who still want to make just a little space in their lives for beautiful things. This book will, I hope, show how even a simple vase of flowers can transform the look or mood of your surroundings if the flowers themselves, the container, the colors and textures are all carefully and imaginatively combined. My formal floristry training was important, but it is much more a matter of having a natural knack for these things, an instinctive feel for what is right, that has guided and inspired me over the years. This is what I have tried to share with you in this book, so that wherever you live or whatever your lifestyle, flowers can be part of your everyday life if you want them to be.

Jane Packer

Vibrant, clashing colors – scarlets, vermilions, crimsons, shocking pinks, sapphire blues, sherbet oranges, acid yellows, and lime greens – capture the spirit of city life. Whether you use them in harmonizing shades of a single color or in startling, breathtaking combinations, flowers in the city should always look strong and contemporary. You can use flowers to create many moods – elegant, chic, ethnic, exotic, serene, or sophisticated – all to enhance their surroundings. Use them to bring out the colors in a nearby painting or to complement a collection of objects.

city

Flowers particularly suited to metropolitan living have strong shapes and definite personalities – tulips (*Tulipa*), roses (*Rosa*), ranunculus (*Ranunculus*), gerbera (*Gerbera*), amaryllis (*Hippeastrum*), and orchids (*Cymbidium*) all fit the bill. Add vegetables and fruits that accentuate the color and texture of the flowers, to create arrangements that have a bold sense of spontaneity and an exciting, cosmopolitan quality. For containers, use anything from brilliantly colored art deco vases to simple, galvanized metal buckets. If your chosen container isn't waterproof, simply hide a glass jar inside it. Be as daring, innovative, experimental, quirky, or original as you wish – anything goes in the city.

Vibrant colors immediately conjure up the bustle and clamor of the city, whether you use them in bursts of a single, vivid shade or create glorious mixtures of color. Things that you see as you stroll through the streets can inspire all sorts of flower arrangements – the bright pinks, yellows, and reds of the ribbons here could be recreated, say, in a clashing display of ranunculus. Lemons in a contemporary wire basket are the perfect accompaniment for a simple flower arrangement for a city kitchen.

When you choose containers, think of the shapes and textures that you see around you in the city. Choose a sleek chrome pitcher to suggest the sophistication of New York, say, or an art nouveau urn to remind you of Paris. Capture the atmosphere with clean, sharp colors, such as white hellebores with bright blue, as shown here; or reflect the blur of city colors with masses of vibrant flowers. Using flowers and containers imaginatively, you can re-create the excitement and exhilarating atmosphere of city life, especially if you keep the arrangement simple and only use one or two varieties of flower.

Gerbera and peppers

Above: Choose flowers and vegetables that match the colors or culinary theme of a dinner party. For Mexican food, for example, try an arrangement of red or orange bell peppers.
Right: This striking arrangement uses a limited number of flowers for maximum impact.
Opposite: Here, shown clockwise from top left, you can see the delicate red stripes on the petals of a long-stemmed French tulip; the raspberry-colored center of a gerbera; the furry green calyx of a gerbera; and the hand-painted quality of snapdragon petals.

The vivid, sometimes shocking colors of the city are brought to life in the exuberant display of flowers and vegetables shown on the following pages. This is an ideal arrangement to make if you're rushing off to buy the food for a dinner party and you want to choose the flowers at the same time. In this case, the flowers and vegetables were both bought from a street market.

I chose a bold color scheme to accentuate the intense coral of the walls – using the luscious, clashing colors of hot pink "Fredigor" gerbera (*Gerbera*), bright yellow "Strahlenkrone" goldenrod (*Solidago*), and golden-lemon French tulips (*Tulipa*). To unify the color scheme, I included a few orange "Debutante" snapdragons (*Antirrhinum*), whose petals are speckled with the yellows and pinks of the other flowers. The glossy yellow peppers in the basket heighten the color of the tulips and goldenrod, and bring out the warm tones in the walls.

This arrangement will last for several days, provided you condition the flowers first by cutting 1 inch off the bottom and placing them in clean water and flower-food. French tulips are more expensive than their English and Dutch cousins, but their long, elegant stems make them ideal for stylish displays like this. Over 500 different varieties of gerbera are available, in a vast range of colors from yellow to burgundy. Sometimes, tulip and gerbera stems go droopy, so trim the base, then wrap the stems in sheets of newspaper and leave them up to their necks in a bucket of tepid water and flower-food for several hours. Prop them upright to prevent the stems from hardening into a position that is difficult to arrange.

When using fruits or vegetables in an arrangement, make sure they fit in with the overall scheme – by choosing either colors that harmonize with the flowers or shapes that echo their forms. You might wrap purple-green cabbage leaves, for example, around a container filled with purple delphiniums (*Delphinium*) and heather (*Erica, Calluna,* or *Daboecia*), or you could insert whole, glossy green apples into a display of spherical, green silkweed seed heads (*Asclepias physocarpa*).

For this display, I filled the wire basket with yellow peppers but you could use whichever fruits or vegetables are in season. Try to keep the top and bottom halves of the arrangement in scale – large-headed flowers may look ungainly if combined with small vegetables at the base. If you can't find a suitable wire basket, use a large glass tank or an attractive wire container instead with a smaller vase placed inside it.

1 Condition the flowers as described on page 14. Fill the inner container with water, place it in the center of the wire basket, and surround it with yellow peppers. Arrange the tulips first, inserting them on one side of the vase only and letting them find their natural position. Their curving stems will help to give a sense of movement.

2 Add several long stems of goldenrod on the other side of the vase, so that its feathery flowers contrast with the sculptural tulip heads.

3 Next, arrange the snapdragons, cutting their stems to varying lengths so they fill the display.

4 Finally, add the gerbera, grouping them in the center of the arrangement so they form a focal point.

Opposite: It is important to look at your own surroundings and then to use them as the basis for your choice of flowers. The original inspiration for this arrangement was the coral color of the walls, which is emphasized by the flowers and peppers. The quirky wire basket complements the unusual metal banisters.

Narcissus tree

A topiary tree like this is a stylish decoration for a city lunch table or an office reception area, yet it looks equally good on a hall table at home. It is easy to make and, if you keep the container topped up with fresh water, it can last for many days. You will have to buy several bunches of flowers to make this tree, so choosing blooms that are in season will ensure that it is still fairly inexpensive. When selecting a container, make sure it will hold the stems tightly and can withstand the weight of the flower heads without toppling over. If your container is porous, hide a glass jar inside it and cover the top with a blanket of carpet moss.

The tree shown here uses "Tête à Tête" narcissus (*Narcissus*), which I love for their miniature, delicate flower heads and their delicious scent. These are complemented by a dark green drinking glass, which accentuates the butter-yellow of the flowers as well as the intense green of the stems. This tree has a contemporary feel, but for a pretty, feminine gift suitable for Mother's Day, you could use "Paper White" narcissus in a pink ceramic pot. A romantic tree, on the other hand, might incorporate jewel-colored anemones (*Anemone*), placed in an ornate metal container and tied with a velvet ribbon to emphasize their heavily pollened centers. These are good examples of how your choice of container can transform the look and mood of a flower.

To extend the life of your flowers, first condition the stems by cutting off 1 inch from the bottom, to remove any cells that have dried out, then give them a drink of clean water to which you have added some flower-food. Leave them in a cool place for a couple of hours, and they will be ready to use. This basic advice applies to all flowers, not only narcissus.

To assemble the tree, mass the stems together in your hand until the flowers form a ball. Try to make as many flower heads as possible face outward. Keep all the stems parallel to form the trunk of the tree, then secure them just beneath the flower heads with garden twine or raffia. This can later be concealed by a decorative ribbon if it suits the style of the arrangement. Trim the bottom of the stems level so they stand upright, then place them in your chosen container.

Opposite: Narcissus are ideal for this type of arrangement, but other flowers with full heads and strong stems can be used instead. For a cheerful, Provençal breakfast room, you could combine sunflowers (*Helianthus*) with a tall terra-cotta pot. If the pot is porous, place a jar inside, concealed by a layer of moss. White "Ludwig Dazzler" amaryllis (*Hippeastrum*) in a square glass tank filled with shells or pebbles would enhance the minimalist atmosphere of a contemporary room decorated in neutral tones. **Left and above:** Color combinations that you see every day in the city can provide the inspiration for an exciting flower arrangement.

Festive garland

Garlands are a traditional element of winter celebrations, especially when they are highly decorated and arranged next to a blazing log fire. But you can make them in many other styles – exotic, contemporary, or elegant – according to the foliage and colors you choose.

In the main photograph on page 23, I've kept the classic festive color scheme of red and green, but given it a modern twist with the glaucous green eucalyptus (*Eucalyptus*) garland and the vermilion chili peppers. To complement the elegant, spacious room, the only

decorations on the mantelpiece are the two dark green vases. The red stone motif that decorates one of the vases is echoed in the branches of scarlet holly berries (*Ilex aquifolium*), which have been stripped of their leaves. Splashes of strong color are provided by the cluster of ruby-red chili peppers on the mantelpiece and the bowl of chilies and sprays of rosemary (*Rosmarinus officinalis*) in the hearth. As the eucalyptus and rosemary leaves dry out, they will release their spicy fragrance into the air – a traditional element of many festive arrangements.

Before you make a garland, you should think carefully about which foliage to use. If the garland is intended to last for a week or more, there's no point in using very soft foliage, such as ivy (*Hedera*), that will soon wilt, wither, or drop. Although berried ivy has woody stems which last longer out of water than plain ivy leaves, it still has a relatively short life. Instead, you should choose leaves that will stay the course, such as eucalyptus, rosemary, or blue pine (*Pinus*). You can choose from about 20 different varieties of eucalyptus, and several varieties of pine, so you can mix them to get a particular look. Blue pine has a rounded shape, for instance, while Douglas pine (*Pseudotsuga menziesii*) has much longer needles. Another idea is to make a garland from bare branches that you have sprayed gold or silver, or which are covered in moss or lichen.

Top: The fuzzy, rounded shape of the blue pine forms a sharp contrast with the clean, vertical lines of this staircase.
Above: The glossy chili peppers emphasize the dual textures of the rosemary leaves – their shiny surfaces and matte undersides.

Above: Berried ivy is very bushy, making it a good choice for a simple, but sophisticated, garland to hang on a plain white staircase.
Opposite: Choose berries or foliage for the way their color, texture, and shape affect the character of the garland.

1 You will need some sturdy string and a spool of florists' wire. Decide on the length of the finished garland, then cut the string to this length, adding 4 inches to each end. Make a loop at each end to allow for hanging, then twist the florists' wire around one end to secure it.

2 The width of the garland is determined by the length of the foliage. For a garland 4 inches wide, you need foliage 8 inches long because you bind the foliage to the string halfway down each stem. Place a stem of foliage on one end of the string and use the wire to bind it to the string, wrapping it around several times so it really bites into the stem. Do not cut the wire as it will be used to bind the next piece.

3 Take a second stem of foliage and bind it onto the previous piece, making sure the stems point in the same direction. Fan it out so that the head covers the stem of the first piece. This hides the wire and strengthens the garland – if you were to bind the foliage directly onto the string, the garland would flop at this point and look awkward when displayed.

4 Continue in this way until you reach the end of the string. Then trim the wire and weave in the loose end.

Opposite: The scarlet holly berries, the searing red chili peppers, and the crimson stones on the vase bring zest to this garland by picking up the warm tones of the berried eucalyptus.

Lilies

I adore the calm, ethereal grace of white arum lilies (*Zantedeschia aethiopica*). To me, they always look best when used with only one or two of their leaves – anything else detracts from their beauty. Lilies are especially suited to spacious rooms in which they make a big impact by standing out from their surroundings. Here, they are placed alongside a birdcage containing nothing but two ostrich eggs, which emphasizes the elegance and purity of the room.

Arum lilies are available throughout the year. They are expensive, but you don't need many for a stunning display, and they are long-lasting. Check their stems from time to time, as they tend to split and curl up after a few days in water. This doesn't matter in ceramic containers, but it is very visible in clear glass vases where the stems play such an important part in the overall effect, so they should be trimmed whenever necessary. Cloudy water will also be obvious, so it is best to change the water every day. Choose an opaque glass vase if a daily change isn't possible.

These arums have no scent, but white longiflorum lilies (*Lilium longiflorum*) and the large-flowered "Casablanca" lilies both have heady fragrances.

The serenity evoked by the neutral tones of the walls and fireplace is enhanced by the timeless quality of the lilies and the clear glass of the vase.

Arrangements don't have to be placed in a vase. Here, for instance, a selection of beautiful squashes is combined with eucalyptus seed pods (*Eucalyptus*) that highlight the subtle and varied colors of the vegetables. When used like this, the pods will dry out and last for weeks.

A variety of squashes and gourds in interesting shapes and colors is available throughout the year, and in the fall orange pumpkins are on sale everywhere from supermarkets to country roadsides. For a room with a predominant theme of oranges and yellows, you could arrange several small pumpkins in an irregularly shaped wooden bowl and drape them with sprays of scarlet berries, such as rowan (*Sorbus aucuparia*). If the room is decorated in warm, spicy tones, you might place the same pumpkins in a beaten copper dish and add a few golden fall leaves.

You can group all kinds of objects together to complement an interior or to form a pool of color on a table. For a Fifties-style living-room, you might arrange acid yellow starfruits (*Carambola*) on a shiny black plate; for a dining room in cool shades of green, group purple figs with globe artichokes on a stone dish lined with grape leaves.

Texture plays an important role in unifying this display. The smooth, steely-blue sheen of the squashes is emphasized by the metallic dish, and their irregular skins are complemented by the knobbly blue seed pods.

Pale pumpkins

Green flowers and foliage

Green flowers are delicate, subtle, and sophisticated. Each year, commercial growers develop new, green varieties of familiar flowers. For this arrangement, in which the green tones of the flowers bring out the various greens in the vases, I chose trailing green "Shamrock" chrysanthemums (*Chrysanthemum*), long-stemmed "Mount Everest" chincherinchees (*Ornithogalum thyrsoides*) with their greenish-black domed centers, and the weird, hairy puff-ball seed pods of silkweeds (*Asclepias physocarpa*).

To fill out the arrangement and provide contrast with the rounded flower shapes, I added the tall, lime-green spires of bells of Ireland (*Moluccella laevis*) and sprays of orange-red hypericum berries (*Hypericum*). All the flowers and foliage in the vase have a long lifespan, provided you add flower-food to the water and change it completely every four to five days.

Other green flowers and foliage that would be suitable are "Envy" zinnias (*Zinnia elegans*), love-lies-bleeding (*Amaranthus caudatus* "Viridis"), guelder roses (*Viburnum opulus*), hellebores (*Helleborus viridis*), and lady's mantle (*Alchemilla mollis*).

Left: This arrangement echoes the collection of mottled green vases and objects.
Opposite: Tulips behave much better when they're allowed to fall quite naturally in a vase.

The bold personality and clean lines of these red and pink tulips (*Tulipa*) instantly evoke a city atmosphere, which is enhanced by the yellow wall behind them and the graphic style of the tray on which they sit. Tulips are good-natured flowers and, if they're conditioned in the basic way, will last for up to a week. If their stems are floppy when you get them home, trim 1 inch off the bottom, then wrap them in newspaper, and leave overnight in a bucket of water and flower-food.

This wicker basket demonstrates that containers don't have to be nonporous. Wicker is often considered to be suitable only for rustic settings, but this basket proves that the shape and weave of the wicker, plus the flowers used with it, determine its mood. Here, the arrangement of the tulips disguises the fact that the flowers are actually sitting in a glass bowl inside the basket. Hiding the real container inside a decorative object gives you plenty of scope for combining different textures and colors. As a centerpiece for a Chinese meal, why not fill a bamboo steamer with Chinese lanterns (*Physalis franchetii*), screw pine (*Pandanus*), and chili peppers?

Overleaf (clockwise from top left): "Paper White" narcissus, silkweed seed pod, hellebore, "Rococo" parrot tulip, lilac, allium, pink tulip, widow iris.

Mass of tulips

Halloween dinner

Pumpkins are usually associated with a country atmosphere, but for this arrangement I wanted to give them the dash and vibrancy of the city. I chose sprays of orange and green ornamental chili peppers (*Capsicum*) for one pumpkin and orange mini-gerbera (*Gerbera*) for the other, because their bold colors and rounded shapes complement each other so well. You need flowers with strong personalities for this arrangement – anything soft or delicate wouldn't stand up to the sharp, contemporary look.

Mini-gerbera have only been developed in the last few years, yet they are popular already because their small size makes them so versatile. They are available throughout the year, but if you can't find them, try the larger ones such as "Fabio" and "Terramexico." Alternative flowers include burnt-orange Iceland poppies (*Papaver nudicaule*), pot marigolds (*Calendula officinalis*), or carnations (*Dianthus*).

This arrangement is easy to make. All you do is slice the top off a medium-sized pumpkin and scoop out the flesh, then fill it with water and flowers.

Opposite: Pumpkins are readily available in many shapes and sizes.
Right: These rich, glowing colors are warming on chilly, winter nights.
Overleaf: For a modern twist to a traditional theme, candlelit baby pumpkins with names carved on them make perfect place settings.

posy swathed in tulle, but balk at one wrapped in crisp sheets of newspaper and tied with thick string?

The wrappings you choose for the posy will affect its mood by emphasizing a flower's color, shape, or personality. You can buy paper in a vast range of textures and colors – from glossy tissue to crinkly crêpe paper or the smooth, shiny, brown variety – or you can use fabric, such as muslin, burlap, stiff net, or silk. And remember that the way you fold the paper or fabric is important, too. The highly scented posy of mauve

Posies

Although the word "posy" conjures up images of something traditional, small, and feminine, posies can also be bang up-to-date, large, dramatic, and a riot of clashing colors.

When choosing the flowers for a posy, it is important to consider the character of the person who will be receiving it. Do they go for dazzling color clashes, or would they prefer a posy in harmonizing tones of a single color, such as the one shown right that combines velvety roses (*Rosa*) in shades of terra-cotta and sand? Would they be delighted to receive a

Opposite, above: For maximum drama, cream amaryllis, scarlet tulips, crimson "Only Love" roses, and laurustinus leaves are wrapped in brilliant red tissue paper.

Opposite, below: The faded terra-cotta of the "Leonardis" roses harmonizes beautifully with the burnished sand color of the "Sahara" roses.

Left: The blue crêpe paper around this posy picks up the lettering on the store bag, which contains a gift.

Below: The lime green luggage tag throws the matching green lady's mantle, bright yellow daffodils, fuchsia pink roses, and deep coral nerines into sharp relief.

"Hugo Koster" lilac (*Syringa vulgaris*), deep purple "Ostara" hyacinths (*Hyacinthus orientalis*), and lime guelder roses (*Viburnum opulus*), shown above, has been wrapped in midnight blue crêpe paper, which has been folded in half and then gathered to form a full, rounded ruff. You can also be inventive when tying the posy – choose from string, raffia, ribbon, garden twine, tulle, chiffon, brocade, or silken cord.

True tied posies have stems that are spiraled (as shown on page 47), but if you are making a small posy, you can simply cluster the flowerheads together in your hand, interspersing them with foliage, and tie them with garden twine.

Proteas and dates

Wrapping fabric around a container is a quick way of making it harmonize with flowers, by highlighting either the textures or the colors. Here, I used several linen napkins for a casual look that brings out the olive-green of the dates (*Phoenix dactylifera*) and the yellows and oranges of the proteas (*Leucospermum cordifolium*). For a special occasion, you could arrange some stately pink-and-white king proteas (*Protea cynaroides*) in a container wrapped in red velvet or brocade and tied with a silken cord.

Neither the dates nor the proteas need special conditioning. Proteas are expensive but very long-lasting and will even dry naturally in the vase once the water has evaporated.

1 Wrap the container in the napkins, folding them so each color is visible.
2 Tie the napkins in place with raffia.
3 Fill the container with water, then position some branches of ornamental dates to hang over one edge. Make a feature of their heaviness by letting them arrange themselves naturally.
4 Now add the proteas to fill the arrangement. They have very stiff stems, so cut them short enough for their heads to rest on the rim of the container.

Opposite: Close-up, we can appreciate the proteas' subtle variations of color.
Overleaf: The primary colors of the flowers are matched by the brightly colored glasses.

Decorative wreaths

The gold ribbons of this blue pine wreath, the warm colors of the dried orange slices, the preserved tangerines, the cinnamon sticks, and the pine cones, all conjure up a festive mood. It also carries the added bonus of a wonderfully rich, spicy aroma.

Wreaths make marvelous decorations, whatever the season. You can create a dense, highly decorated one for a traditional interior, like the elaborate wreath shown on the left, or make airy, contemporary wreaths, such as the ones on the facing page, using the minimum ingredients in settings in which a sense of simplicity is important.

Wreaths are ideal for many different occasions – from winter festivals to summer outdoor celebrations. The blue pine wreath has a winter theme, with its bundles of spicy-scented cinnamon sticks and preserved oranges. Heavy decorations like these need to be held in place by a substantial base, so cover a metal wreath-frame with moss or straw – a floral foam base would be too flimsy.

The base of the simple wreath of white "Athena" roses (*Rosa*) is made from young, pliable branches – try stripping the leaves off branches of honeysuckle (*Lonicera*), forsythia (*Forsythia*), or dogwood (*Cornus*). First spray them all over with antique gold paint, then coil them into a wreath shape, holding the branches together with little twists of florists' wire. Aim for a slightly wild look – the escaping branches give a sense of movement and form a filigree effect. The little test tubes are bound with gold wire for a simple, understated look. I filled each one with clean water and a single rose, but you could use a white anemone (*Anemone*), gardenia (*Gardenia*), or camellia (*Camellia japonica*) instead.

The classic wreath of salal leaves (*Gaultheria shallon*) has an elegant, architectural look. It is made on a moss-covered, metal wreath-frame. These are sold in various diameters, although it is best to choose a small one because very large frames look funereal when decorated in this simple way. Choose your foliage according to how long you want the wreath to last. Bay (*Laurus nobilis*) is a good choice because, even though it will dry out, it will still look attractive. Other options are preserved magnolia leaves (*Magnolia*), which you can buy ready-glycerined and dyed, or preserved copper beech (*Fagus sylvatica*).

To make the salal wreath, start by covering the frame with sphagnum moss (see page 43). This is used to line hanging baskets, so it is widely available from florists and garden centers. If you can't find it, use a floral foam wreath base instead. The leaves are pinned on individually, using "U" pins – small lengths of florists' wire bent into hairpin shapes. Decide which is the top of the wreath and start there, turning the wreath counter-clockwise as you work, so the first pins are covered by the next layer of leaves. These are pinned on near the base of the first leaves, and the second pins are hidden by the following layer of leaves. Keep turning the wreath counter-clockwise as you add leaves. When you have finished, pin on a simple bow – anything ornate will detract from its classic lines.

Above: The antique crystal chandelier, the raw texture of the simple wreath, the delicate roses, and the test tubes create a serene, contemporary look that is perfect for the city.

Left: This intricate wreath of overlapping salal leaves is set off by its simple surroundings – the plain matte-finished wall and the white candle pots. It wouldn't look right against a heavily patterned background.

Citrus and chili wreath

The design and colors of this vibrant wreath are just right for decorating a home in the city. The scarlet chili peppers clash with the bright orange chilies, tangerines, and kumquats, and with the fuchsia-pink raffia. The wreath looks particularly arresting set here against the backdrop of a bright purple front door.

A dazzling wreath like this is the perfect way to welcome your guests to a celebratory party, especially if you continue the theme inside the house with arrangements in the same vivid colors or containing the same ingredients. Table decorations to accompany this wreath could consist of small, conical topiary trees covered with kumquats and placed in scarlet ceramic pots, or cerise vases filled with vermilion and orange ranunculus (*Ranunculus*).

When you make an arrangement like this, it's important to choose perfect fruits and vegetables because any damaged or bruised produce will quickly start to go moldy. The wreath will last for several weeks if left outdoors in cool weather, but it will soon deteriorate indoors or in warm climates, so you should make it only the day before you need it, and store it overnight in a cool place.

This wreath makes a vivid color statement that you can continue inside the house. For a less extrovert version, combine green tulle with green apples and green chili peppers.

1 You'll need a wire wreath frame, sphagnum moss, a ball of string, a length of raffia, and 7-inch-long florists' wires, plus red and orange chili peppers, kumquats, and tangerines.

2 Wire up the fruits and vegetables. The tangerines are fixed to the wreath with two wires, due to their weight. Push the wires into the fruits at right angles to each other, then twist them together at the base to make four legs. Smaller fruits and vegetables, like the kumquats and chili peppers, need only one wire, twisted at the base to make two legs.

3 To bind to the sphagnum moss, first tie the string onto the frame. Tease out a handful of moss and pat it into a long cylindrical shape. Place this over the wire base and bind the string around it, pulling it taut toward you so the moss is firmly attached to the base. If it is too loose, the moss won't support the weight of the tangerines and they'll sag or fall off – the heavier the ingredients, the more compact the moss should be. Continue in this way until the wreath is covered. Fasten off the string.

4 Twist the raffia around the wreath and hold it in place with florists' wires bent double into "U" pins. To do this, hook a "U" pin over the top of the raffia and down through the moss, twist the two legs around at the back, and tuck the sharp ends back into the moss.

5 Attach clusters of fruits and chili peppers with wire, working with the largest pieces first. Hold the wires at the base of each fruit and feed them through the moss, then pull them out back of the wreath. Twist the legs around each other firmly and push them back through the moss. The fruit theme can be continued indoors, as here on this candle.

Hanging tulips

It's traditional to hang ornaments on your tree at Christmas, but why not hang up a few flowers instead? This inventive table centerpiece, with its sharp reds, cool lilacs, and deep pinks, is a world away from a conventional festive decoration, which would seem completely out of place in such modern surroundings. The classic color scheme of red and green is still there, but I've given the arrangement a contemporary twist with the glass container, suspended test tubes, and the pink-and-purple oxidized metal bowls.

As for the flowers, I used scarlet amaryllis (*Hippeastrum*), variegated pink roses (*Rosa*), plus crimson and lilac tulips (*Tulipa*). Amaryllis are deservedly popular flowers at Christmas, because their generous, velvety trumpets look marvelous in a wide range of settings. Here, I used "Red Lion" amaryllis but there are several other red varieties to choose from, including "Red Velvet." Amaryllis have long, thick stems which florists often support internally with thin sticks or canes. I've solved that problem here by cutting the stems very short. This immediately alters the personality of the flowers, transforming them from tall, elegant blooms into cheerful bursts of vivid color.

The "Matisse" roses are splashed with deep and pastel pinks, making them look like raspberry-ripple ice cream. These beautiful speckles form a refreshing contrast with the deep red of the amaryllis. The pale pinks of the roses go with the elongated lilac tulips, and the yellow-fringed petals of the crimson "Rococo" parrot tulips marry with the gold stamens of the amaryllis.

I placed the flowers in a square, glass tank, which unites them with the test tubes hanging above the arrangement. These were tied to a central light fixture above the table, using red-and-lilac nylon twine. For more color and pattern, I criss-crossed the twine down the barrels of two of the test tubes, and then twisted red twine around the outside of the glass tank to continue the theme.

You'll see that I've also hung tulips in test tubes on the Christmas tree. They might not last for the whole of Christmas, but they'd look spectacular for a special party.

For a fresh, contemporary look, attach the test tubes with shiny or iridescent nylon twine that catches the light. When making a feature of a few flowers in this way, choose perfect specimens because any faults or flaws will be clearly visible.

Bridal bouquet

Above and overleaf: Changing fashions in bridal dresses have affected the popularity of many flowers, but roses are an enduring favorite. There's a vast range of colors and shapes to choose from, with many new roses being introduced every year. Commercially grown roses used to lack scent because the gene associated with fragrance restricts the flowers' longevity, but commercial growers are now breeding roses that enjoy the best of both worlds.

I've lost count of the number of weddings I have worked on over the years, and yet I always base my choice of flowers on a few cardinal rules. No matter how pretty or radiant, a bride will only look her best if her flowers match the style of her outfit, complement her skin tones, and suit her personality. She may look fantastic carrying a single cerise lily (*Lilium*) tied with a huge ribbon, or she may have the coloring and image that suits the bouquet shown here, made from porcelain pink "Valerie" and off-white "Athena" roses (*Rosa*), and no other foliage at all.

Whenever I talk to a bride about the flowers for her bouquet, I always ask about the entrance she hopes to make. Does she want to turn every head or would she prefer to look demure and virginal? I also ask about her outfit, because this determines the shape of the bouquet or posy. A flamboyant, tied posy of several varieties of flowers, with long tendrils of ivy and jasmine, looks spectacular set against a huge-skirted wedding dress. Something understated, on the other hand, calls for a smaller, sophisticated posy, with no more than two varieties of flower and one type of unusual foliage – such as hosta (*Hosta*) leaves – forming a ruff around the

outside. An elegant, figure-hugging dress requires an equally *soigné* bouquet – roses in every shade of red from the scarlet "Jaguar" to the near-black "Baccarolla" would look divine.

Color is a major consideration. White is still very popular, of course, but many brides are now going for much stronger colors. In the winter, for instance, when bold colors make a dramatic statement against the cool, wintry palette, you could make a romantic posy of dark purple anemones (*Anemone*) tied with matching velvet ribbon. Replacing these with white anemones or Christmas roses (*Helleborus niger*) and finishing off with a white bow would radically alter the look to one of purity and freshness.

Before you make the bouquet, it's important to condition the flowers properly. Roses, especially, need careful conditioning, as they are notorious for developing drooping heads, caused by an air-lock in the stems. You can avoid this by conditioning them as soon as you get them home. But, please, resist the temptation to smash or crush their stems. Although it's claimed that this increases their ability to take up water, it also encourages bacteria to enter the stems and this reduces the life of the flowers.

1 It's essential that you condition roses as soon as you get them home.

2 To condition correctly, use a sharp knife to strip off every thorn along the whole stem and all the leaves below the binding point. Trim off the bottom 2 inches of stem at a sharp angle, to expose the maximum surface area to the water, then wrap in newspaper, and leave to stand in a bucket of cool water and flower-food for at least two hours.

3 Choose the flowers that will form the center of the posy – here, three roses. Tie on a length of soft string or green garden twine at the binding point. To determine the diameter of your bouquet, choose the position of the binding carefully. For example, for the bouquet to be 12 inches in diameter, your binding point should be 6 inches down the stems.

4 Begin to add more flowers at this point. Add them one at a time, wrapping the string over each stem and rotating the bouquet in a counter-clockwise direction as you do so. Continue until you've formed a complete circle around the central flowers, then build up a second tier of flowers. As you work, grip the stems as tightly as possible, to ensure the bouquet is tight and the flowers are held firmly in place.

5 As you add the next tier of flowers, begin to slant the stems at an angle, so as to create an even, domed shape, but always keep the binding point in the same position. The stems will start to spiral outward. When the bouquet is complete, tie the string securely, and trim the bottom of the stems level.

6 Immediately place the bouquet in water until required, then wrap the stems in your chosen fabric. Here, I've used a long swathe of tulle.

Festive mantelpiece

Opposite: I've used dark green ivy and lime green pears, apples, and grapes to contrast with the white walls but you should choose whichever colors suit your decor. In a green or red room, for instance, you could create an opulent effect with dark green ivy, red grapes, and green globe artichokes. If your walls are bright blue, on the other hand, little pyramids of oranges, tangerines, and kumquats would form a striking contrast.

Candles, fruits, and ivy are traditional decorations for a winter mantelpiece, but I wanted a fresher look here to suit a contemporary room. Keeping the basic ingredients, I've created a lively garland full of movement, by winding long trails of ivy (*Hedera*) between gold, silver, and cream candles in all shapes and sizes – cones, corkscrews, and classic church candles. This random selection of shapes and sizes transforms what might otherwise be a formal display into something much more spontaneous.

1 Group the candles on the mantelpiece. Place them in deep glasses, cups, and bowls so they won't fall over. Choose the taller containers carefully, as they will be visible in the finished display.

2 Wind long ivy trails around the candles so that they trail over the edge of the mantelpiece, then arrange the fruit in between.

3 To frost some of the fruits and ivy, dab on small splashes of white acrylic paint.

4 Leave to dry, then burnish with small smears of gold or silver acrylic paint.

Valentine heart

Valentine's Day is an exceptionally busy time of the year for florists everywhere, and it's also extremely stressful – everyone wants the flowers to arrive at a particular time, often at the same time! And since so many people only buy their flowers at the last minute, I have to make sure I order enough to meet the demand without being left with a massive surplus.

The whole flower-growing industry works hard to make Valentine's Day a success, not only in producing the millions of flowers that are needed but also in improving the quality of the blooms. Throughout the year, for instance, technologists strive to lengthen a flower's lifespan and performance, while nurseries develop and perfect dazzling new varieties.

For many people, red roses (*Rosa*) are still the classic choice for Valentine's Day. It is because they have become so popular and widely available that I constantly look for inventive ways of wrapping and displaying them to their best advantage. A simple bunch of long-stemmed red roses, such as "Jacaranda" or "Baccarolla," looks sumptuous with masses of tissue paper in a Hollywood-style gift box, tied with a lavish bow. You can create drama with black tissue paper or an invigorating, contemporary look with hot oranges, crimsons, or pinks.

If you are looking for an alternative to the ubiquitous rose, then other suitable red flowers include freesias (*Freesia*),

amaryllis (*Hippeastrum*), tulips (*Tulipa*), anemones (*Anemone*), and gerbera (*Gerbera*). Scarlet carnations (*Dianthus*), which are sometimes regarded as the poor relation of the flower world, look wonderfully glamorous when wrapped in swathes of tissue paper and placed inside a long, elegant box.

Dried flowers are the answer if you want an arrangement that will keep, especially if you buy the new freeze-dried flowers which, although expensive, retain their color like fresh flowers (see pages 68–9). The dried-flower heart shown opposite is the perfect choice for a romantic memento and it's very easy to make. Just cut the stems below the bud and glue them into a heart-shape of flower foam. You'll need about 50 roses for a base 7 inches wide.

Opposite: The sugar-pink tissue paper enhances the bluish-red of the roses.
Top, above and left: Although red roses (left) are still a firm favorite for Valentine's Day, more people are seeking alternatives. While red tulips (top) are an elegant substitute, a classic topiary tree of dried roses in a terra-cotta pot (above) makes a more lasting memento.

The countryside has always been a great source of inspiration for me, so when I opened my first flower shop, I tried to re-create a little corner of the country in the heart of London. Floristry was still rather traditional and formal then, although the whole country look was beginning to infuse it with new life and freedom. My idea of a country-style arrangement is one in which the flowers look as if they've just been cut from the garden, even if they were commercially grown and bought from a florist. I would choose simple, unpretentious flowers with open faces, rather than

country

tight buds, and soft, rather than stiff, stems. Marigolds (*Calendula officinalis*), cornflowers (*Centaurea cyanus*), hollyhocks (*Alcea*), cosmos (*Cosmos bipinnatus*), poppies (*Papaver*), sunflowers (*Helianthus*), and some roses (*Rosa*) all have the right character, and look especially good when mixed with other flowers and foliage. Choose greenery that could have been picked from the hedgerow or garden, and include other rural ingredients as well, such as catkins, pine cones, rose hips, and fruits. For containers, the more informal and the older they are the better. Pitchers, teacups, and sugar bowls all fit the bill, as do woven or twig baskets and lichen-covered flowerpots, provided they complement their informal, relaxed surroundings.

Wicker is a classic country texture, but it doesn't
have to look contrived or "ethnic." You can fill a
sophisticated plastic-lined twig basket with pots
of growing plants, such as primroses (*Primula
vulgaris*) or violets (*Viola odorata*), and cover
the tops with sphagnum or bun moss. Twig and
wicker wreath bases also have a strong rustic
feel, whether you use them in their original
state or whitewash them first. You can also use
wreath bases made from straw.

The country look is essentially very natural and pure. Choose simple flowers, such as daffodils (*Narcissus*), which could easily be found growing in grassland or a flower bed. Country flowers can have full and abundant flower heads, such as peonies (*Paeonia*) and ranunculus (*Ranunculus*), or be small and delicate, such as snowdrops (*Galanthus*) and poached-egg flowers (*Limnanthes douglasii*). Reflect this fresh atmosphere by decorating interiors with cotton, linen, and muslin fabrics, rather than silk or velvet.

Country style needs to have a "lived-in" look. Distressed paint finishes, which would look quite wrong in a sophisticated city-style interior, create a sense of warmth and relaxation in a country setting. Choose containers with distressed surfaces, such as old wooden or woven baskets or aging terra-cotta pots, combining them with delicately colored flowers and interesting foliage. Scented flowers, such as honeysuckle (*Lonicera*), roses (*Rosa*), and lily-of-the-valley (*Convallaria majalis*), evoke the countryside – if you've walked through a bluebell (*Hyacinthoides non-scripta*) wood, you will remember the delicious, spicy fragrance. Sadly, bluebells don't last long in water but you could re-create their blue haze with forget-me-nots (*Myosotis*) or grape hyacinths (*Muscari*).

Spring collection

In the early days of spring, when winter seems reluctant to loosen its grip, one of the best ways to cheer up a room – and yourself – is with a bunch of brightly colored flowers. Even if the yard is looking bleak and empty, florists will always have a wide selection of flowers in glowing shades of yellow, orange, and red. Among others, you can choose from ranunculus (*Ranunculus*), daffodils (*Narcissus*), broom (*Genista*), mimosa (*Acacia dealbata*), anemones (*Anemone*), freesias (*Freesia*), sunflowers (*Helianthus*), and gerbera (*Gerbera*).

This small pitcher of apricot tulips (*Tulipa*), orange pot marigolds (*Calendula officinalis*), silkweed flowers (*Asclepias tuberosa*), and a few nodding catkins (*Salix*) is an ideal choice for early spring because the colors are so fresh and sharp. Note how the chartreuse leaves of the marigolds and silkweeds marry with the green stripes on the tulips and the green centers of the marigolds. This is the sort of color association I really enjoy making – choosing one flower or leaf that brings out the delicate details of another. For this reason, always take a close look at your flowers and foliage before arranging them.

Consider the setting, too. Relaxed meals in the country call for equally informal flowers and containers, which is why this simple arrangement works so well. This is the time to bring out your favorite pieces of china – pitchers, sugar bowls, teacups, coffee-pots, and even

soup tureens. Don't worry if they're slightly chipped – less-than-perfect china can look charming and adds to the atmosphere. For a centerpiece, try to pick a fairly short container which, when filled with flowers, won't obscure your guests' view of one another – there's nothing worse than having to peer around a huge display every time you want to talk to someone!

All the flowers and foliage in this arrangement have roughly the same lifespan and will last for about 10 days, provided they're conditioned properly (see pages 154–6).

Another appealing combination for a spring lunch table could include purple and yellow hellebores (*Helleborus lividus*), purple reticulata irises (*Iris reticulata*), and branches of fluffy yellow kerria flowers (*Kerria japonica*).

Opposite: The vibrant color scheme of this pitcher of spring flowers will brighten up the dullest of mornings.

Above: This close-up of a marigold shows its lime green center and the surrounding ring of red-tipped petals that seem to have been individually lacquered.

Afternoon tea

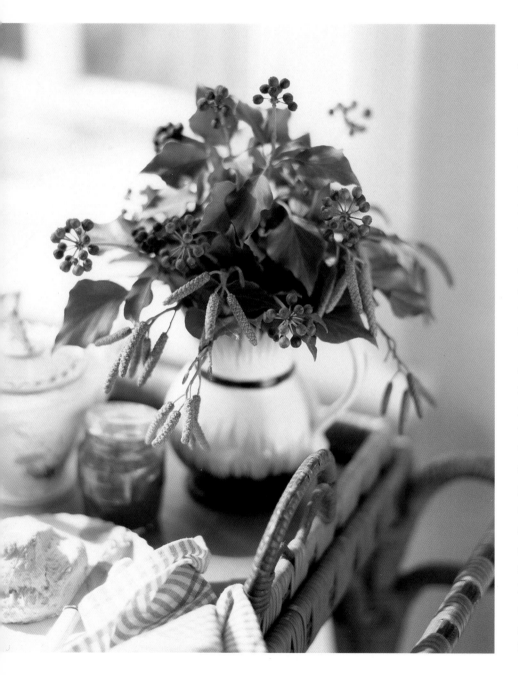

Ever since I opened my first shop I've offered a good selection of foliage because it can add so much to an arrangement – either as a filler or to set off existing elements. Here, I've used nothing but foliage – ivy (*Hedera*) and catkins (*Salix*) – but you only realize this when you take a second look, because the star-shapes of the ivy berries and the long tendrils of the catkins permeate it with color, life, and movement.

The colors of this pretty, Fifties pitcher set off the green and black leaves, berries, and catkins, and, more generally, it suits the informality of the display and the nostalgic, tea-time setting.

This is the sort of arrangement that can be picked from the garden at the last minute, just before your guests arrive. If you don't have a garden, florists stock a wide range of ornamental foliage, whatever the season. Attractive berried foliage includes cotoneaster (*Cotoneaster*), pyracantha (*Pyracantha*), honeysuckle (*Lonicera*), viburnum (*Viburnum*), and skimmia (*Skimmia*). In summer, choose from a wide variety of scented herbs, such as rosemary (*Rosmarinus officinalis*), lemon balm (*Melissa officinalis*), parsley (*Petroselinum crispum*), mint (*Mentha*), and my favorite – scented geranium leaves (*Geranium incanum*).

Shape and form play an important role in this arrangement, where the rounded ivy berries contrast with the weeping catkins and glossy, diamond-shaped ivy leaves.

Daffodils are among the easiest flowers of all to arrange, which may be the reason they're so popular. Their radiant colors and glorious scent are wonderful heralds of spring and I think they look particularly arresting arranged on their own in a pitcher or vase.

For this arrangement, all I did was trim their stems to roughly the same length and put them straight into a glazed yellow pitcher. Although they need little in the way of adornment, I placed a little cup and saucer of orange roses (*Rosa* "Tennessee") behind them, which highlights their orange trumpets.

Until a special flower-food was developed recently for spring flowers, daffodils would kill off any other flowers that were mixed with them. This is because daffodil stems release a sticky sap that's poisonous to other flowers – you'll have seen it for yourself whenever you've cut a daffodil stem. In the past, you had to put the daffodils in conditioning quarantine by leaving them in fresh water for 24 hours before mixing them with other flowers. Now you can use a special flower-food instead that does the job for you. To prolong the life of your daffodils, remember to trim the base of the stems to remove any dried-out fibers.

The shape of this pitcher sets the showy daffodils off to perfection, but for a more contemporary look, try displaying them in a decorative metal watering can.

Pitcher of daffodils

Cool kitchen greens

Many kitchen implements and containers are so attractive nowadays that they often serve a decorative purpose as well as a practical one. If you collect old-fashioned tinware or interesting china, this is a good time to draw attention to it by filling it with flowers and foliage that accentuate its color and set off its shape.

For this kitchen arrangement, I used green cottage tulips (*Tulipa*), "Paper White" narcissus (*Narcissus*), and some cream silkweed flowers (*Asclepias tuberosa*), all of which came from my flower shop. To enhance the informal, country feel of the arrangement, I also included a few wispy sprigs of foliage picked from my own garden. These are long trails of variegated "Angularis Aurea" ivy (*Hedera helix*) – which I used to soften the outline of the display – as well as some sweetly scented tendrils of silvery lavender (*Lavandula angustifolia*), which pick up the soft dove-gray of the vase and form a spiky contrast with the smooth, almost sculptural, shape of the tulip flowers and leaves. In the summer, you could combine the same foliage with white, scented "Haytor" or "Mrs Sinkins" pinks (*Dianthus*), white peonies (*Paeonia*), and the delicate, nodding stems of white bleeding hearts (*Dicentra spectabilis alba*).

Whichever flowers you choose, don't forget to strip off any leaves that will sit below the water line, otherwise they'll quickly turn soft and mushy and make the water go cloudy.

Opposite and above: When combining lots of different ingredients in a display, it's important to have a central theme. In this pitcher, I've used a color scheme of green, gray, and white.

Bedroom roses

Cutting down the stems of a flower can totally transform its look and character. The "Champagne" roses (*Rosa*) I've used here usually appear, still tightly in bud, in tall, sophisticated arrangements. In contrast, I've cut the stems right down, placing them in a tiny glass vase just as their heads are opening, so they look as if they've only just been picked from the garden. Delicate blooms such as these need little adornment – here, a collar of pink-tinged laurustinus buds (*Viburnum tinus*) completes the effect.

This style of low arrangement is perfect for a bedside table, a windowsill, or the top of a chest of drawers, as it carries a sweet perfume that lingers over many days. I often make similar displays for my children's bedroom, combining stems of foliage with grape hyacinths (*Muscari*), ranunculus (*Ranunculus*), or early primroses (*Primula vulgaris*) in a rustic ceramic jug. Another simple idea is to float a single flower head in a small dish or to combine it with other delicate blooms in an egg cup or coffee cup for a charming, but understated, display.

Left: Low arrangements like these are a good way of using up flowers whose stems are broken, or which are the only survivors from a larger arrangement.
Opposite: The open heads of the coral pink roses pick up the streaks of pink in the centers of the anemones in this traditional arrangement for a country bedroom.

Dried arrangements

Mixed arrangements of dried flowers, such as pink larkspur (*Consolida ajacis*), pink love-in-the-mist (*Nigella damascena*), and burgundy love-lies-bleeding (*Amaranthus atropurpureus*), sometimes look rather dull and traditional. A more contemporary approach for a stylish country look is to use only one color and type of flower in a container that coordinates with the flowers and the surrounding decor. For this feature, I've filled a trio of painted terra-cotta pots with dried lavender (*Lavandula angustifolia*), roses (*Rosa*), and hydrangea heads (*Hydrangea macrophylla*).

Containers obviously play an important role in creating the right sort of look – some wicker baskets, for example, can make an arrangement look contrived and clichéed. For alternatives, choose a basket with a distressed paint finish, a weathered stoneware jug, or a painted flowerpot. For a contemporary, country room, try putting a pot of dried lavender inside a square glass tank filled with scented lavender potpourri.

There are many different methods of drying flowers. Flowers can often be dried at home but a popular commercial technique is known as freeze-drying, which, although more expensive than traditional techniques, produces stunning results because the blooms retain their color and intensity. Whichever way you choose, make sure you use the flower foam specially formulated for dried flowers.

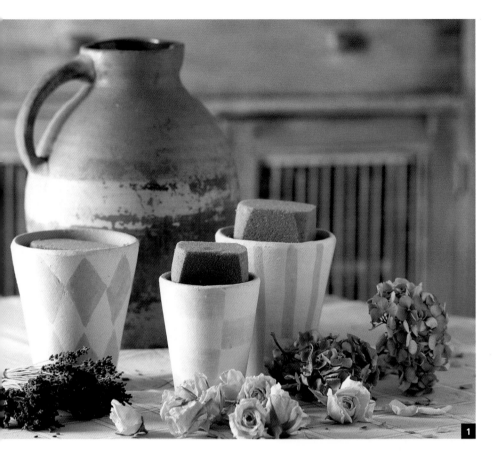

Opposite: These pink, yellow, cream, and red freeze-dried rose heads look as if they've just been picked. Their colors are still strong and vibrant, and their petals haven't withered in the way that air-dried flowers do. The result is very fresh and natural.

Overleaf: The colors of the lavender, roses, and hydrangea heads are slightly muted to match the simple, relaxed atmosphere of the room and the distressed surface of the tall jug on the table. The painted pots provide extra interest and pattern, and form the link between the three very different arrangements.

1 Cut blocks of brown flower foam to shape, and push them down into the pots. The foam in the center pot and on the right stands proud because the finished arrangements will have a domed shape.

2 Next, prepare the flowers. The hydrangeas are not wired, but pushed directly into the foam. The roses are wired singly and the lavender is wired in bunches. Ensure the lavender heads in each bunch are level, then trim the stems to varying lengths to create the graduated dome effect. To wire the stems, twist a length of florists' wire around the stems several times, then pull down to form two "legs." Build the arrangements by inserting one row of flowers across the foam first and another at right angles to it, then fill each quarter with flowers.

Pots of roses

The simple shapes and sharp, clear colors of these pots of roses (*Rosa*) bring dried flowers bang up-to-date. I chose these painted pots because they harmonize so beautifully with the warm tones of the roses and the mellow grain of the wooden table. For a fragrant display, add a few drops of essential oil to the dried flower foam before inserting the flowers. Choose a single oil, such as lavender, rose-geranium, or ylang-ylang, or a commercially blended one that is specially produced for scenting rooms.

Pots of dried flowers make excellent gifts, especially if you choose flowers and containers that match the mood and colors of the recipient's home. A good choice for someone with a boldly colored kitchen, for instance, would be a mass of dried red and orange chili peppers in a decorative terra-cotta pot. Or you could use some of the new, freeze-dried fruits that are now being sold. To make a dried arrangement for a minimalist interior, try filling a stone container with dried poppy (*Papaver*) or scabious (*Scabiosa*) seed heads. At Christmas, dab the sere heads of dried lace-cap hydrangeas (*Hydrangea macrophylla*) with gold acrylic paint and arrange them in a gold-painted pot, then tie a raffia bow or a simple muslin or paper ribbon around the rim.

These pots of freeze-dried roses are made in the same way as those shown on pages 70–1. Using different roses and containers creates a country look that's warmer, yet still modern.

Bunches of mixed flowers hanging up to dry are an integral part of many country kitchens, but here they've been given a contemporary twist. Instead of using a random mixture of flowers and grasses, which would have a far more rustic character, I've concentrated on fat bunches of lavender (*Lavandula*), which I've hung up with lengths of chunky rope for added texture and interest. Few flowers are more evocative of the countryside than lavender, and its heady scent makes it perfect for freshening up a stuffy kitchen. You can easily re-create this look, whether the lavender you hang up has been picked from your own garden or bought from a florist.

Lavandula angustifolia is a very good-tempered plant and doesn't object if you cut off all its flowers in late summer. In fact, this is an excellent way of keeping it in shape. Sadly, the pink and white varieties of lavender aren't so amenable and their flowers don't dry at all well. White lavender, in particular, can look quite dirty, and more dead than dried.

Several other flowers look attractive when hung up in bunches in the kitchen. Try blue-flowered rosemary (*Rosmarinus officinalis*), trails of clematis (*Clematis alpina*), dried cornflowers (*Centaurea cyanus*), or blue delphiniums (*Delphinium*).

Hanging fat bunches of lavender from varying lengths of chunky rope, alongside pots and pans, looks suitably informal and relaxed for today's country-style kitchens.

Lavender

Simple topiary trees

Opposite and above: Patience is needed to make a topiary tree from small dried flowers, but the results are worth it. Here, I've used baby yellow chrysanthemums for the single tree and white "The Pearl" achillea for the trio of trees.

Topiary trees have been popular for many years, but for this feature I wanted to create something different from the traditional mix of dried flower heads. For a stylish look, I've limited my choice of flowers to one variety and kept to a single color scheme. I used baby yellow chrysanthemums (*Chrysanthemum*) for the single tree, and white "The Pearl" achillea (*Achillea ptarmica*) for the trio, but other suitable flowers include love-in-the-mist seed heads (*Nigella damascena*), poppy seed heads (*Papaver*), roses (*Rosa*), and larkspur (*Consolida ajacis*).

The trunk should look as natural and interesting as possible – whether it's cut from the branch of a real tree, has a gnarled vine twisted around it, or is made from a handful of cinnamon sticks. It should complement the mood and color of the flowers and container, as well as the setting. For a tree of dried pink roses, you might place a trunk of silver birch in a pewter or silver bowl. To enhance the rich tones of a wooden table, on the other hand, the tree might consist of a studded head of ruby rose hips and a stem of cinnamon sticks placed in a copper bowl.

Decide how big you want the tree to be, bearing in mind that sprigs of lavender (*Lavandula*) 2½ inches long, for example, will add 5 inches to the width of the top of the tree. The size of the head will also influence the size of the container you use. Ideally, the decorated head of a round topiary tree should be at least as broad as the pot. For a conical tree, the widest point of the head should match, or be slightly bigger than, the widest point of the pot. Personally, I prefer the trees to be squat rather than elongated – but this is a matter of taste.

Once you've made these decisions, the trunk must be secured in its pot. You can either push it into a piece of dried flower foam cut to fit the pot, or hold it permanently in position with quick-drying cement or plaster. The top of the foam or cement can be disguised with lichen moss glued into place. Create the foundation for the head of the tree by binding more moss into the required shape with spool wire or pushing a sphere or cone of dried foam down onto the trunk. You are then ready to add the flowers. For all the trees shown here, the flowers were wired up in bunches before being inserted into the foam.

1 To wire a small bunch of flowers, take medium-gauge florists' wire and lay it on top of the stems, halfway down. Hold it in place between thumb and forefinger and pull both ends down to make two "legs." Wind the leg nearest to you around the stems and the other wire several times to hold them in place, then pull it down. To create a perfectly spherical tree, insert a band of flowers around the circumference of the tree.

2 Insert a second band at right angles to the first. Finally, fill in each quarter in turn to cover the foam entirely.

Mixed border display

Although I actually bought these flowers from a flower market, they could easily have been picked from a mixed border in a garden. It's the glorious mixture of flower varieties and colors that creates this impression – a combination that would look equally at home growing in a lush, herbaceous border in a country garden. The warm tones of the flowers complement the russets, grays and yellows of the container – a yellow ocher urn that is perfect for this magnificent country arrangement.

To continue the garden theme, I picked traditional open-headed flowers, including cerise peonies (*Paeonia*), gold double ranunculus (*Ranunculus*), deep blue cornflowers (*Centaurea cyanus*), tomato red "Nikita" spray roses (*Rosa*), and single terra-cotta "Vicky Brown" roses. To highlight the sunny glow of the ranunculus and introduce a feathery texture, I added yellow yarrow (*Achillea filipendulina*) and the acid green flowers of lady's mantle (*Alchemilla mollis*). I also used a few taller flowers to add height and contrast with the rounded shapes of many of the other flowers, including deep purple stocks (*Matthiola incana*) and hot pink snapdragons (*Antirrhinum majus*), with a few sprigs of crimson love-lies-bleeding (*Amaranthus atropurpureus*) trailing over the front of the container.

Instead of using floral foam or crumpled chicken wire to hold the stems in position, which can be fiddly to insert and cause the stems to split, I arranged

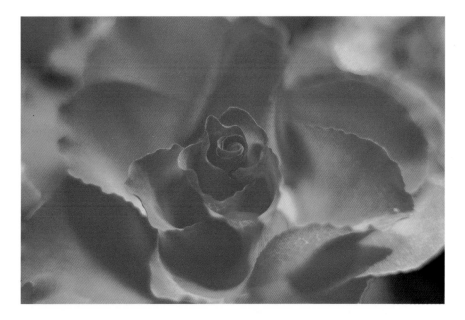

the flowers in a narrow plastic container hidden inside the urn. The flowers trailing over the rim hide the inner container from view.

The arrangement is built up in tiers, starting with the flowers trailing over the sides of the urn and finishing with the tallest elements in the middle. For a spontaneous look, let the flowers find their own natural positions, rather than forcing them into artificial shapes. The love-lies-bleeding, for instance, will drape itself into elegant curves, as will the "Nikita" roses.

Many summer flowers are short-lived, particularly stocks and peonies, so it's best to make an arrangement like this only a few hours before you need it. To get the most out of the flowers, buy them when they're still in bud but showing some color, otherwise they may

never open. This is especially true of peonies, which won't open if they're bought in tight green bud with no other color visible.

To get the best out of stocks, choose them carefully. They have very crumpled and dry-looking leaves, which can make them look as if they're dying. It's the color, rather than the texture, of the foliage that you should check, however – fresh stock leaves are a strong sage green, and are covered with a slight down.

Opposite: If you want to increase the fragrance of this arrangement and ensure it lasts as long as possible, replace the peonies with lilies.
Above: The "Vicky Brown" rose is a relatively new variety. It looks particularly effective in country-style arrangements because its faded color makes it look like a garden rose.

Nostalgic arrangement

Successful arrangements don't have to involve armfuls of flowers – this simple display uses only three "Vivaldi" roses (*Rosa*), yet, because they've been chosen so carefully to match the containers and their surroundings, they really enhance the mood of the setting.

Here, the faded yellow-pink of the "Vivaldi" roses combines with the sepia tones of the antique bottles and the deep mahogany wood of the mirror frame to create a nostalgic still-life that would look completely at home in a country bedroom.

When re-creating this arrangement, take care that you use bottles or other containers of varying sizes and shapes, to give the arrangement a sense of spontaneity and prevent it from looking too uniform. Placing the bottles in front of a mirror will give them added impact, especially if they're very small.

Other antique-looking flowers particularly suited to this kind of display include pale yellow freesias (*Freesia*), old-fashioned pinks (*Dianthus*) or cream Californian poppies (*Eschscholzia*). Do remember that if you're picking roses fresh from the garden, it's best to gather them early in the morning before the sun reaches them and starts to fade their delicate blooms.

The combination of faded damask "Vivaldi" roses, an old mahogany mirror, and antique bottles creates a nostalgic arrangement for a country bedroom.

Not every room benefits from a complex flower arrangement. Some country-style interiors, for instance, look best when decorated with a plain pitcher of simple flowers or a vase of one variety only. This modest dining room, with its country furniture and collection of silver objects, needs only a few well-placed flowers as anything exuberant or flamboyant would look completely out of place. These white ranunculus (*Ranunculus*) fringed with pink look charming set against a plain off-white wall, which emphasizes their elegant, serpentine stems and delicate coloring. Even though the other silver containers don't contain any flowers, they extend the arrangement and complement the galvanized metal churn that has been used as a container.

Ranunculus look best when they're allowed to fall freely in a container and arrange themselves naturally, which is exactly what happened here. Alternative flowers for a simple setting like this one include any daisy-like flowers, such as marguerites (*Argyranthemum frutescens*) or white China asters (*Callistephus chinensis*), or astrantia (*Astrantia major*). Pale pink sweet peas (*Lathyrus odoratus*), with their curved tendrils, would be another good choice.

Ranunculus are extremely long-lasting, which is one of the reasons why I like them so much. You may find the single-colored bunches more expensive than the mixed bunches, but at least you can enjoy them for a week or more.

Churn of ranunculus

Warm kitchen reds

Both of the arrangements on pages 84–5 rely for their impact on the vivid colors and bold shapes of the flowers, and on the way they perfectly complement their simple surroundings.

My starting point for the first arrangement of gerbera (*Gerbera*) and ranunculus (*Ranunculus*) was the collection of china and glass with its black-and-red rooster motifs. I like to draw attention to special collections like this by choosing flowers that enhance the colors and shapes. The eye-catching blood red "Beauty" gerbera and ranunculus used here are perfect partners to the naive rooster motifs that decorate the pitcher and tumblers.

Gerbera and ranunculus are among my favorite flowers, not only because they look so bright and cheerful but also because they're available in such a vast range of striking colors – from those with black, green, or yellow centers to ones with a central frill of petals that contrasts with the color of the outer petals. They are sold as single and double flowers, and a new variety has shaggy petals. Over 500 different varieties of gerbera are currently available, with new ones appearing all the time, so it can be difficult for florists to identify a particular variety. If you want to order a specific color from your florist, it may be easiest to give him or her a color swatch of paper or fabric which can then be matched with the gerbera sold by the wholesalers.

Ranunculus has a wonderful animated quality and it is this, along with the bright color range, that gives the flowers an almost child-like appeal. There is a wide variety to choose from. They have single and double flowers and are generally in season from fall through late spring. As well as being sold in single colors, you can also buy bi-colored ranunculus, with central petals contrasting petals, and flowers whose petals are edged with another color.

Both gerbera and ranunculus are long-lasting, although gerbera are prone to wilting unless they're placed in scrupulously clean containers. To prevent the stems going soft after a few days through bacterial attack, add a single drop of household bleach to the water in the vase. Ranunculus are much more easygoing, and will last in water for five to eight days, but they are thirsty flowers so you should top up their water every day and change it completely every three or four days. And always use flower-food in the fresh water.

The mug of scarlet and black "Mona Lisa" anemones (*Anemone*) on page 85 is the simplest evocation of country style. This sort of arrangement is the ideal adornment for an everyday lunch table, and it goes perfectly with the red-and-white checked tablecloth and napkins. It would look equally effective on a windowsill framed by checked curtains. You could change the colors of the anemones to match those of the surroundings – to decorate a hutch containing a collection of blue-and-white china, for instance, place purple and mauve anemones in a large blue-and-white mug, or fill several smaller, antique pitchers with individual flowers and space them at intervals along the shelves.

Anemones are available from fall through early summer, and are sold in inexpensive mixed bunches and in more costly single-colored bunches.

This mug of anemones is easy to make. All you do is gather the flowers together in your hand, as if you were making a posy, placing the tallest flowers in the center and grouping the shorter ones around the outside. When you have an even, domed effect, trim the stems level and then place them in a container of water and flower-food.

Opposite: Pelargoniums are particularly suitable for country arrangements because of their simple shapes and warm colors.

Page 84: The tightly furled petals of the ranunculus contrast with the smiling, open faces of the gerbera. I placed the gerbera lower down in the arrangement and allowed the ranunculus to sit on top of them, so their animated shapes and curved stems are visible.

Page 85: The only foliage is the occasional tendril of anemone leaf that peeks through the clusters of anemone flowers.

Easy country style

The two arrangements on pages 88–9 both use tulips (*Tulipa*) but to very different effect.

Although I've used nothing but parrot tulips in the first arrangement on page 88, the complex patterns of their pink, yellow, and green streaked petals create plenty of color and interest. Their fresh green leaves match the apple-green vase, and the flowers light up their dark surroundings in a way that's reminiscent of paintings by Dutch Old Masters. More often than not, arrangements that have been inspired by these paintings are rather elaborate and grand, containing a wide variety of flowers and trailing fruits. Here, however, I've achieved a more countrified look by simplifying and dividing the flowers and fruit – the tulips are arranged in one vase and a dish of burgundy grapes sits behind them. Another, more sophisticated, interpretation of this theme for the fall would be to combine a vase of deep red, late-flowering clematis (*Clematis*) and purple-fruited trails of brambles (*Rubus*) alongside a plate of greeny-purple cabbage leaves, piled high with globe artichokes or green gourds.

It's unusual to see tulips cut so short – parrot tulips look like hot-house blooms when treated like this. To prepare them, condition them in the usual way by cutting off at least the bottom inch of stem, then leaving them in tepid water and flower-food for a couple of hours. After this, you can cut down their stems to the required length and strip off any excess foliage. Then place them in your chosen vase, arranging them in layers. Start with the shortest stems, resting their heads on the edge of the container, then insert each layer in turn, so the flowers support one another.

For the arrangement on page 89, I chose flowers that would enhance the colors of the rusting table top. The red tulips, streaked with yellow, and the catkins (*Salix*) do this perfectly, and the rosy apples draw the eye to its rust-flecked surface. The result is an informal display that creates a relaxed atmosphere. These catkins come from the willow family but several other plants produce them, including the silk-tassel bush (*Garrya elliptica*) which has long gray-green catkins in late winter and spring, and the corkscrew hazel (*Corylus avellana* "Contorta") which bears yellow ones on bare, twisted branches.

This arrangement would work equally well on a weathered painted surface, where the top coat of paint has flaked off to reveal a contrasting undercoat. To harmonize with your own surroundings, choose flowers that complement the different colors in the paintwork of a table, dresser, or bookcase. For green and red distressed paintwork, for example, you could combine scarlet roses with damson plums or raspberries, and for paint with yellow overtones, use marigolds (*Calendula officinalis*) and lemons.

The scent of lilac (*Syringa*) (see page 90) is highly evocative of gardens in late spring, when its heavy, spicy fragrance fills the air. Sadly, lilac doesn't last very long when picked from the garden, because all the plant's energy has been directed into producing its heavenly perfume. Commercially grown lilac lasts longer but at the expense of its scent, which is lost altogether. To ensure that lilac lasts as long as possible, strip off all the lower leaves, trim the stems at a sharp angle, then place the branches in a bucket of tepid water and flower-food for a few hours. Contrary to popular belief, hammering or splitting the stems can shorten the life of the flowers because it increases the chance of bacterial attack.

Opposite: What looks at first sight like the flames of a fire is really the butter-yellow center of a scarlet tulip.

Page 88: These parrot tulips seem to glow against the dark backdrop of burgundy grapes.

Page 89: The red-and-yellow tulips, with the catkins and apples, create a mellow and warming still-life on a rusting table top.

Page 90: The empty enamel pitchers expand the arrangement without using extra flowers.

Page 91 (clockwise from top left): The fragile petals of a "Sterling Silver" rose; the ruffled petals of a white ranunculus; the individual flowers of lilac, and some green catkins streaked with the same pink as the lilac.

Riot of ranunculus

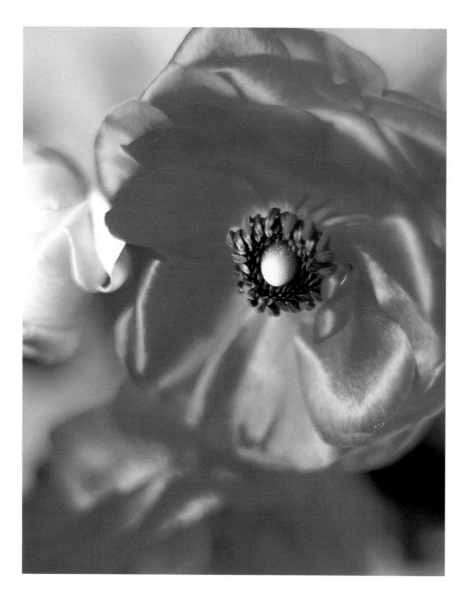

Ranunculus (*Ranunculus*) are among the chameleons of the flower world. They can look bold and voluptuous, as shown here, or delicate and modest like the ones in the arrangement on page 81.

This riot of clashing colors is ideal for this sunny, brightly colored living room as it intensifies the yellows, reds, and blacks in the tablecloth and the surrounding objects. The result is a cheerful, country arrangement that's just right for its relaxed summer setting.

When you buy mixed bunches of ranunculus, like the ones shown here, you'll usually find that some flowers have already opened while others remain in tight bud. Rather than burying the buds in the center of the arrangement where they become lost, I made a feature of them here by placing them so they curve upward in gentle arcs and stand out against the fully open flowers. Some of the long, curving stems trail lazily over the sides of the vase, breaking up what would otherwise be a dense mass of flowers and giving the arrangement a sense of movement.

When you create an arrangement like this, let the flowers support themselves in tiers. Cut the first layer short so they rest on the rim of the wide-shouldered vase, then build up the other flowers in layers, letting them arrange themselves whenever possible. Choose the colors as randomly as you can to give the arrangement a sense of spontaneity in keeping with the relaxed country setting.

Opposite: This Fifties-style vase brings glamour to these ranunculus. By cutting the stems short, the vivid colors are intensified by concentrating them at one level.
Above: The shiny petals of this ranunculus look like the flounces of a Fifties satin ballgown.

Serene still-life

First impressions are made in people's hallways, so it's important to think about what sort of atmosphere you want to create or enhance with your flowers. Ideally, they should set the tone for the rest of the house, so you need to decide whether to create a shocking statement with a riot of vibrant, clashing colors, or something more modest and serene with an array of delicate, understated blooms.

For this hallway, I chose a harmonious arrangement of gently toning flowers to match the serene aquamarine walls. Choosing flowers in varying shades of one pale color creates a restful effect as the eye is drawn from one vase to the next. The result is a continuous drift of color which looks interesting because of the different flowers, tones, and textures involved. The flowers I selected include purple lilac (*Syringa*), pale purple snapdragons (*Antirrhinum*), pale lilac roses (*Rosa* "Blue Moon"), purple foxgloves (*Digitalis purpurea*), the lower leaves from the foxgloves, and mauve stocks (*Matthiola incana*). Together, they release a delicious and soothing fragrance – another bonus for a hallway, where first impressions are so important.

Perhaps the obvious arrangement for these majestic summer flowers would have been a large single-vase display. Although that would have looked equally stunning, I wanted to do something personal and interesting here. Placing different flower varieties in their own container not only creates a

continuous and varied display across the whole sideboard, but is also an excellent way of showing off a special collection of containers. Here, I've used pitchers and vases in harmonizing shades of aquamarine.

You can see that I've resisted the temptation to fill every container – placing a handful of foxglove leaves in one pitcher or leaving the occasional vase empty adds interest and stops the arrangement from becoming cluttered.

The arrangement will last for several days, provided you keep the containers topped up with fresh water. The foxgloves and snapdragons are very long-lasting, although you may need to pick off the flowers from the lower stems as they start to wither. You could even replace some of the flowers in the smallest vases with stems that have survived from a larger display.

Opposite: It isn't necessary to fill every vase or pitcher in your collection. You'll see that I've left one or two empty ones to draw attention to the containers themselves and prevent the display from looking too "busy."

Left and below: Foxgloves and snapdragons, with their bell-shaped flowers, complement each other well. Up close, the exquisite markings of the foxglove can be appreciated.

Bedside table

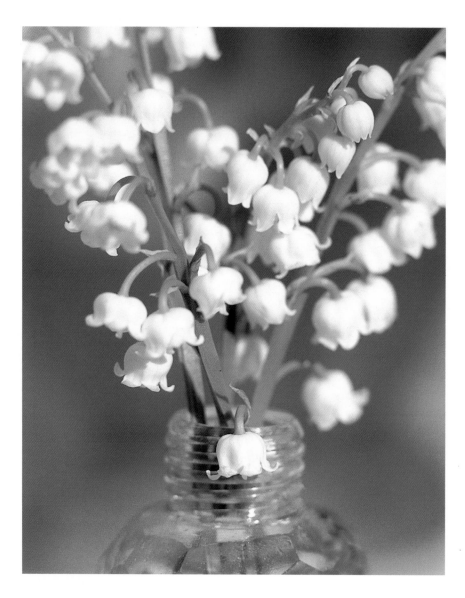

Opposite: Part of the charm of this arrangement lies in the combination of antique glass and jewelry with old-fashioned flowers.
Above: Sometimes the smallest container makes for the perfect arrangement – here, this delicate cut-glass perfume bottle is just right for the miniature sprays of lily-of-the-valley.

Fragrant, delicate arrangements are perfect for the intimacy of a country bedroom, and especially for the bedside table where they can be seen up close and their fragrance enjoyed last thing at night and first thing in the morning.

Whatever the color of your bedroom, white or cream flowers promote a sense of peace and serenity. Here, I've contrasted the voluptuously large heads of white "Duchesse de Nemours" peonies (*Paeonia*) and some cream stocks (*Matthiola incana*) with the dainty bells of lily-of-the-valley (*Convallaria majalis*). The arrangement is made soft and feminine by cutting the peony stems short and letting them rest on the rim of the container. I allowed the stocks to drape themselves gently over the edge of the vase, to further soften the shape of the arrangement and create a sense of ease and tranquility which is, of course, ideal for the sanctuary of the bedroom.

The frosted vase would have looked great on its own, but the addition of a small glass bottle of lily-of-the-valley adds charm and character. These are highly fragrant, and their size makes them just right for miniature containers.

Unfortunately, fully open peonies do not live long in water, so this arrangement would be perfect for a guest's bedroom. Longer-lasting alternatives include "Mrs Sinkins" pinks (*Dianthus*), lisianthus (*Eustoma grandiflorum*), or scabious (*Scabiosa*).

You don't have to live by the sea to re-create the wonderfully serene atmosphere of a cool seashore in your home. The key is simplicity and harmony – there are no vivid or jarring colors here, only the pale, soft shades of blues, sea-greens, and silver-grays. For texture, think of rounded shells, sea-smoothed driftwood, gnarled, salt-encrusted rope, and undulating sand. Flowers, while still a valuable part of the overall scheme, do not dominate or overwhelm these arrangements. An understated cluster of daisies or a single white gerbera in the right context have all the qualities needed for this

sea

utterly simple look. And these arrangements can look good wherever you live – they are particularly suited to the relaxing atmosphere of the bedroom or the privacy of the bathroom where motifs such as shells or starfish, and soft, cool colors often decorate the interior. Among the flowers you can use to re-create this look are silver-blue sea holly (*Eryngium*), lavender-blue speedwell (*Veronica*), dried white yarrow (*Achillea filipendulina*), white and pink flowers of chives (*Allium schoenoprasum*) which look like sea thrift (*Armeria maritima*), pale pink scabious (*Scabiosa*), silver-blue foliage of lavender (*Lavandula angustifolia* "Hidcote"), feathery love-in-a-mist (*Nigella damascena*), and silver-green lamb's ears (*Stachys lanata*).

The photographs on this page capture the spirit of the sea – the feeling of calmness and well-being that often steals over you as you gaze across the sands. You bring this spirit into your home by making arrangements that incorporate the textures, colors, and shapes of the seashore. Twist rope around your container, cement a pattern of stones into a wall or on the side of a terra-cotta pot, or use a piece of driftwood as a stake for a plant. Choose flowers that look as if they've just been picked from a sand dune and surround them with a few pretty pebbles, some shells, or a pale yellow sand starfish or green sea urchin.

The sea can be exhilarating, with its crashing waves, intensely blue sky, sparkling spume, and the play of sunlight on the water. Go for colors that recreate this freshness – cobalt blue on paler blue, sun-bleached shades of green, the browns and rusts of old chains washed up on the beach. For containers, choose crazed opaque glass, aquamarine china vases, or speckled brown pottery.

Sea holly and speedwell

This small still-life instantly suggests the seashore, with its shell, pebbles, rope, and marine blues seen in the color of the enamel plate, the bottles, and the flowers. These different shades of blue echo the pale blue of the walls and the cobalt blue bowl on the table, creating a harmonious look.

Ideally, the ingredients for a sea-style arrangement should look as if they have been gathered on a lazy walk through the sand dunes, and for this reason I chose bottles, pebbles, shells, and lengths of old rope that can be found washed up along the shoreline.

Texture plays an important role in this still-life, where the roughness of the rope and the string that binds the bottles together contrasts with the smooth, glassy pebbles and the sheen of the glass bottles. The flowers, too, contrast in texture – the brittle leaves and jagged thistles of the sea holly (*Eryngium*) stand out against the graceful trailing spikes of the speedwell (*Veronica*) with their soft, feathery leaves.

When choosing flowers for simple, sea-style arrangements like this one, you need only a few flower sprigs. Lavish blooms would look out of keeping with the unassuming nature of the display, and would disrupt the sense of balance and harmony. The blue, thistle-like flowers of sea holly and the tall, nodding plumes of speedwell are ideal as they both look as if they might grow in sparse clumps near the seashore.

Sea holly, as its name suggests, grows naturally by the sea – its spiny, gray-green leaves reflect how Nature has enabled it to withstand very dry, sunny conditions. The distinct shape of the flowers, surrounded by their ruffs of jagged spines, makes sea holly an excellent choice for arrangements in which you use only a few sprigs. Several varieties are available, some much more compact than others, with leaves in varying shades of gray and green. The flowers dry and store extremely well, enabling you to build up a stock of flowers throughout the seasons. Simply tie the stems together with rubber bands and hang them upside-down in a well-ventilated room away from direct sunlight and moisture.

Speedwell is most commonly seen growing in gardens, yet a few spikes in a blue vase are evocative of the sea. It has silvery-green leaves and flowers that range from white to deep ultramarine.

Both speedwell and sea holly are easy to condition. Strip off any leaves that will sit below the water line, trim off the bottom inch of stem, then leave the flowers up to their necks in cool water and flower-food for at least two hours before arranging them.

Instead of sea holly and speedwell, you could use a few spikes of blue lavender foliage (*Lavandula angustifolia* "Hidcote"), purple or pale blue hardy geraniums (*Geranium*), sprigs of wild garlic (*Allium ursinum*), or sage (*Salvia*).

Opposite: This arrangement relies for its impact on the choice of contrasting textures in toning cool blues and bleached creamy grays.
Above: Seen close-up, the delicate spikes of speedwell resemble underwater seaweed.

Each of the vases contains something different, yet all four harmonize with their bleached creamy colors and smooth, rounded shapes. I placed a few cream pebbles in one vase, then added some water so the pebbles would be magnified through the glass and gain a soft-focus quality. Another vase is filled with a collection of pearly shells, including a gray topshell and a small periwinkle. Again, these are placed in water to increase their apparent size and to enhance their iridescent qualities. The other two vases are filled with

Hanging vases

The essence of a cool seashore is captured in these simple hanging glass vases. Suspended from lengths of copper wire, they sway back and forth at the window as if in a gentle sea breeze, with water, copper, and blue-tinted glass glinting in the sunshine. Colors are pale and harmonious, with the combination of pearly, iridescent shells and papery white flowers catching the eye with purity and freshness.

Opposite, above: Choose shells that are large enough to be seen clearly from a distance without being so big that they dwarf the vase.
Opposite, below: The fresh green center and yellow stamens of the white lisianthus flower add just a hint of color.
Left: You could use a few white love-in-the-mist or cosmos flowers instead of this hydrangea.
Below: By placing pebbles in water, you draw attention to their varied and subtle colorings.
Overleaf: Hanging vases in front of a window enhances the luminosity of the glass and flowers. If you don't have an appealing view, use a backdrop of billowing muslin.

flowers – a single white mophead hydrangea (*Hydrangea macrophylla*) in one, and a few papery white lisianthus (*Eustoma grandiflorum*) in the other.

I hung the vases from a curtain pole, where they could sway in the breeze that blows in from the open window looking out on a deck and the sea beyond. You could, however, combine these vases with billowing muslin curtains to create an equally serene look in a city bedroom, say, especially if you hung a couple of suitably atmospheric paintings or posters nearby. The vases would also look good in a bathroom with white tongue-and-groove paneling and a few beautiful shells on the windowsill.

Glass tank with shells

The neutral shades of this unassuming arrangement – the sea-smoothed pebbles, sun-bleached rope, and trachelium (*Trachelium caeruleum*) – embody the nostalgic mood of a wintry seashore.

For a tropical look, combine coral starfish and exotic shells with white scented "Casablanca" lilies (*Lilium*) or apricot "Rilona" amaryllis (*Hippeastrum*).

1 Gather all the ingredients together. You'll need a large, square glass tank with a smaller vase placed inside it, sand, textured rope, shells, and about eight stems of trachelium.

2 Fill the inner container with handfuls of sand, arranging them in heaps to resemble the irregular shapes of dunes. Fill the central vase with cold water.

3 Bury the end of the rope in the sand, then loop the rest loosely around the inner and outer containers.

4 Slide the shells into the cavity between the two containers, placing them at different angles.

Cut trachelium to the same length. Arrange the flowers in tiers, starting with a collar around the outside to conceal the necks of the vases. Add the remaining flowers, packing them in tightly to give an even, rounded shape.

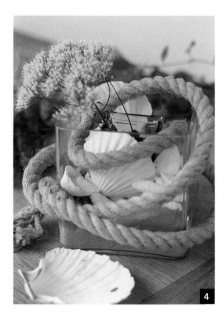

Opposite: The starry heads of the trachelium resemble foaming waves and soften the hard outline of the square tank.

Ethereal orchid

For this arrangement, I've placed a single, white phalaenopsis orchid (*Phalaenopsis*) in a metal basket filled with stones and driftwood, to create an arrangement rich in the silver and white tones you see on a winter seashore. The soft, translucent beauty of the orchid contrasts with the hard, sculptural shapes and textures of the wire basket, stones, and driftwood.

1 You'll need a galvanized metal inner container, a larger metal basket containing some stones, a few gnarled pieces of driftwood, Spanish moss, a length of rope, and a phalaenopsis orchid in a flowerpot.

2 Place the galvanized container inside the basket, adding more stones if necessary to raise it higher. Arrange the driftwood in one corner of the basket.

3 Drape some Spanish moss in and around the basket, weighting it down with stones and driftwood to give the impression of washed-up fishing nets.

4 Place the orchid, still in its flowerpot, in the metal container. Remove the bamboo stake and replace it with a piece of driftwood, tying it in place. Conceal the top of the flowerpot under a blanket of stones and driftwood.

Opposite: Phalaenopsis orchids are very long-lasting but need to be kept in the shade in the summer. Their ethereal quality particularly suits the airy atmosphere of this room.

Utterly simple style

Above: Feathers are used in place of flowers.

Opposite: All the colors and textures in this bathroom can be found on the beach.

Page 116: The white hyacinth flowers are reminiscent of the delicate, waving tentacles of jellyfish, sea urchins, and some seaweeds.

Page 117: Pots of white pelargoniums would also look good in this style of container.

Page 118: The deep blue paint on the fruit box enhances the steely gray of the stones and the silver-green of the marguerite leaves.

Page 119: I chose a single white gerbera because its daisy-like petals reflect the shape of the starfish.

The arrangements on the following five pages reveal how you can easily create a sea style in the home by combining simple flowers with some of the ingredients you would expect to find washed up along the seashore.

If you live near the sea, you can collect suitable shells and pebbles next time you visit your favorite beach, but you can also create the right look in a city interior. All you need is some rope, a few pebbles from the garden, and some attractive shells, sea urchins, sea horses or starfish bought from a shop.

The small still-life shown on the left, consisting of a few feathers, some dried seaweed and a handful of seed pods, could easily be assembled using ingredients collected from a beach. You could sprinkle the contents with scented oil to provide a sea-style alternative to the usual potpourri.

The bathroom shown on the right is decorated in the classic style with an arrangement of favorite sea-style objects. Attention has been drawn to the collection of glass bottles by decorating two of them with sprigs of blue speedwell (*Veronica*). These in turn pick up the blue of the soap and towels, the amethyst-colored shells, and the cornflower blue chair rail, which holds a starfish and some prized shells.

For the white hyacinth bulbs (*Hyacinth*) on page 116, I filled the base of the glass jar with pebbles instead of mud to give them a luminous quality

and tied a length of rope knotted with pebbles around the neck to add individuality and character. If you are growing the flowers from scratch, place the bulbs and stones in the jars and wait for the hyacinths to grow. If you don't have time for this, simply wash the soil from the roots when the hyacinths are in flower and then place them directly into the glass jar.

Beach huts and boats are often painted in cerulean blues to match the colors of the sky and sea. I have re-created this look on page 117 by painting the walls in vivid marine blues and tying the pot of blue hydrangeas (*Hydrangea*) with turquoise nylon cord. This cord is the same color as fishermen's nets and, sure enough, some scallop shells have been caught up in it. This style of decoration is ideal for containers on a seaside patio or deck.

Another idea for a deck is the arrangement on page 118 of white marguerites (*Argyranthemum frutescens*) in a blue-painted fruit box. The flowerpots are covered over with a layer of sand and pebbles. If you want to put the box on a table, you'll have to line it with a thick plastic sheet first so you can water it. Alternatively, you could create the arrangement in an old kitchen sink or drinking trough in the garden.

Less is more in the very simple arrangement on page 119. Here, a single white gerbera (*Gerbera*) is placed in a glass bottle tied with string.

Easy and relaxed, the arrangements in this section are for outdoor living. There are lavish table decorations for summer weddings, both traditional and contemporary table centers for dining alfresco, and fun ideas for a children's party. Even a simple flower arrangement can transform a table setting and enhance the atmosphere for family and friends. To get the right look, choose flowers and containers with care. There are no tight, formal-looking flowers in this section – just large, voluptuous blooms tumbling spontaneously over the sides of

garden

containers, from ceramic vases and plastic tumblers to terra-cotta pots and wirework baskets. Flowers that naturally belong in outdoor settings include roses (*Rosa*), peonies (*Paeonia*), and delphiniums (*Delphinium*). These are popular herbaceous border flowers and crop up time and again in this section, as do forget-me-nots (*Myosotis*), lady's mantle (*Alchemilla mollis*), and China asters (*Callistephus chinensis*). Herbs and vegetables shouldn't be forgotten. In this chapter, you'll find novel displays of globe artichokes, cabbages, and mixed culinary herbs in stylish settings that accentuate their brilliant colors, differing textures, and aromatic fragrances.

Take inspiration for colors and textures from the garden and use containers that are usually found there, such as old galvanized watering cans and buckets that have weathered outside over the years. Or distress new ones by dabbing them with turquoise acrylic paint to imitate the attractive greenish patina of verdigris.

Terra-cotta flowerpots are the obvious choice for garden arrangements, and look especially good if they are weathered and so blend in with the garden. To achieve the same effect with new pots, paint the outside with watered-down natural yogurt and then leave them outside for a couple of weeks.

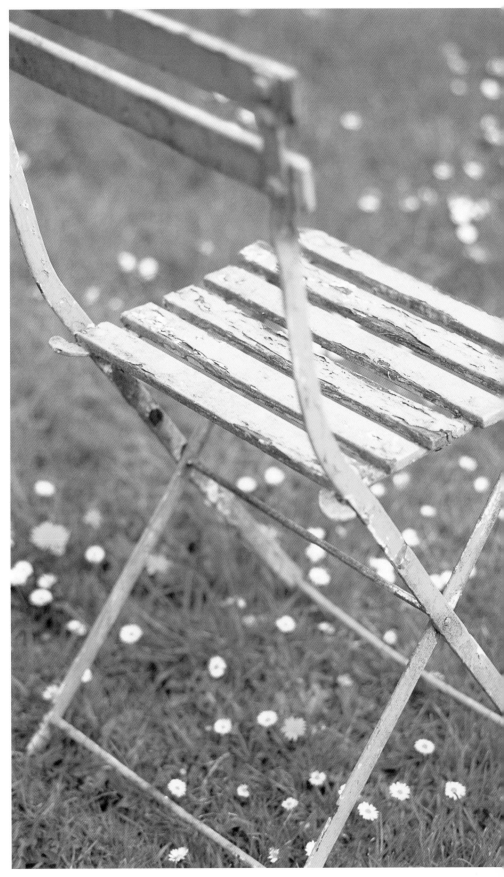

An old picnic table makes an ideal display area for a collection of pots. Massing the pots together in one group – rather than scattering them piecemeal around the yard – and choosing flowers that complement one another gives the display a sense of structure and harmony. The yellow chair shown on the right stands on a lawn studded with daisies and dandelions, a typical garden image that you can re-create in the home by placing small vases of individual marguerites and marigolds on a picnic table.

Pots of herbs

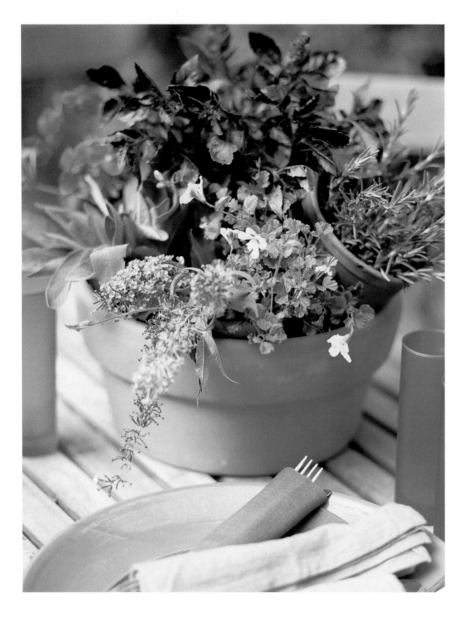

Here, I've created a natural, spontaneous-looking display simply by placing small bunches of cut herbs in miniature preserving jars hidden inside terra-cotta pots and stacking them, in turn, inside a larger pot.

Most flower arrangements have a "look but don't touch" quality. This one, on the other hand, is not only for touching but for eating too. Colorful and aromatic, it's ideal for alfresco meals, where it can be savored and enjoyed for several days. Make it as a centerpiece for a lunch table and the guests can sprinkle the contents on their food or drop them into their drinks. Peppermint (*Mentha piperita*) and chamomile (*Chamaemelum*), for instance, are excellent in tea, while mint (*Mentha*) is used to make the classic mint julep.

I used cut herbs placed in preserving jars hidden inside the flowerpots for this display, but you could easily use pots of living herbs. Mixed arrangements of, say, culinary or medicinal herbs have variety and interest, but single plantings look good too. Golden-leaved marjoram (*Origanum marjorana*) has a bushy, rounded habit, while some varieties of thyme (*Thymus*) look almost like topiary work. I chose a mixture of colors and textures for this centerpiece – purple basil (*Ocimum basilicum purpurascens*), gray-green common sage (*Salvia officinalis*), and silver-green rosemary (*Rosmarinus officinalis*). A few flowers here and there – pelargonium (*Pelargonium*), plumes of purple buddleja (*Buddleja davidii*), and the lilac pink of a scented geranium (*Geranium incanum*) – create little pools of color.

For a completely different look, either whitewash the pots or paint them in colors that complement your china.

1 First assemble the flowerpots. You'll need one large, wide pot and several smaller pots in varying sizes and shapes. You'll also need drinking glasses and glass jars which can be hidden inside the pots. Make a pediment by placing one flowerpot upside-down in the center of the wide pot, then arrange the other pots around it, placing them so that they protrude at varying angles and heights.

2 Place a glass jar or drinking glass inside each pot and fill them with cold water. This may make a mess, so work on a surface that can be wiped down and won't be damaged by the water.

3 Trim the stem of each herb so it will extend out of the flowerpot by about 3–4 inches. You can use herbs cut from the garden, growing in pots, or bought in packs from supermarkets. If you do use garden-grown herbs, however, wash them thoroughly to remove any insects or splashes of soil, and pick off any damaged leaves. Aim for a selection of herbs that will provide interesting contrasts in color and texture – the variegated herbs, for example, are particularly attractive.

4 Begin to arrange the herbs. I started with the topmost pot, as this established the height of the arrangement, but there's no hard and fast rule about this. Don't overfill the vases, or the herbs will hide the terra-cotta pots.

5 Continue to arrange the herbs. I've added a few flowers too, for color and texture. Choose simple, edible flowers, like nasturtiums (*Tropaeolum majus*) or flowers that are considered as herbs, such as pot marigolds (*Calendula officinalis*).

Then just sit back and enjoy the fruits of your labor.

Globe artichokes

The architectural shape of globe artichoke heads (*Cynara scolymus*), which, strictly speaking, are flower buds, makes them perfect for contemporary-style table settings.

This arrangement is very easy to make, although it involves some forward planning as the flowerpots need painting in advance. I chose tall terra-cotta pots because their elongated shape complements the bulbous heads of the artichokes. These were painted dark

green to match the deepest color in the wrapping paper; you can paint yours whatever color seems appropriate.

For an evening dinner party, hollow out the center of each artichoke and fill it with a votive candle. For a sophisticated look, gild the artichokes with gold spray-paint and paint the pots gold. If artichokes are hard to find, use green or purple ornamental cabbages (*Brassica oleracea*) instead. If you leave the roots on, they'll last for several weeks.

Sheets of wrapping paper decorated with globe artichokes make the perfect tablecloth for this arrangement.

Sunflowers (*Helianthus*) have always been popular in gardens and as a staple crop, but until recently they have never lasted long in water – that is, until commercial growers started to produce new varieties of sunflower especially for the cut flower market. Today, sunflowers are available virtually all-year-round and many varieties last for as long as ten days in water.

You can buy sunflowers with brown or green centers, with fluffy heads like chrysanthemums, or with bronze petals.

There's even a dwarf variety called "Teddy Bear" that can be grown in a container or window box.

When buying sunflowers, always choose stems with sturdy green leaves covered with down, and reject any with insipid, pale green foliage. If any of the petals turn brown or start to look ragged after a while, pull them out with your fingers and you'll be left with a huge brown or green center surrounded by a tiny ruff of green leaves, which looks very striking.

A dazzling display of brilliant sunflowers and lime-green lady's mantle (*Alchemilla mollis*) is set off by a matching yellow ocher, glazed earthenware bowl.

Burst of sunflowers

Garden wedding

Wedding receptions and parties are particularly enjoyable when held outdoors – provided, of course, that the weather behaves itself – and this garden, with its magnificent cherry tree in full blossom, is an ideal venue.

When planning the flowers for an outdoor celebration, it's important to look at the setting. If the garden is relaxed and informal with drifts of color and masses of different flower varieties, your best choice is a loose, informal arrangement of mixed garden flowers. If, on the other hand, the layout is formal with neat clipped box hedges and a carefully orchestrated color scheme, you will need equally formal flowers in appropriate shades.

Your choice of flowers and containers should reflect not only the style and color scheme of the garden, but also its scale. This garden is quite spacious, so I could afford to use fairly large flower heads and a dramatic color scheme, both of which prevent the arrangement from being lost in the flower setting. The cherry tree, in particular, forms a focal point in its own right, so I had to be careful that the flowers weren't swamped by it. My choice includes both pastel pinks to harmonize with the tree and shocking pinks that focus the eye upon the table decorations. For containers, I went for large, architectural ceramic pots in azure blues and greens which form a dramatic feature, yet don't detract from the flowers.

Opposite and above: For this summer wedding, I've chosen flowers that traditionally grow in mixed herbaceous borders – delphiniums, peonies, Solomon's seal, astilbe, and foxgloves. The voluptuous peonies, which look like old-fashioned roses, are perfect for informal arrangements.

1 Choose a heavy rope that will stand out against the white tablecloth. You'll also need garden twine, carpet moss, and scissors. For the flowers, I used pink "Sarah Bernhardt," cerise "Félix Crousse," and white "Duchesse de Nemours" peonies (*Paeonia*). Condition the flowers beforehand by leaving them in cool water and flower-food for at least two hours. If the moss has dried out, soak it in water to help keep the flowers moist. Using the string, bind handfuls of the damp moss at intervals along the rope, spacing them so sections of the rope are visible in between. Cut off the string and fasten it securely.

2 Tie the string onto the rope between the clumps of moss, then tightly bind on a couple of "Sarah Bernhardt" peonies.

3 Bind on a "Félix Crousse" peony so its petals just rest against the base of the "Sarah Bernhardt" peonies. Place a handful of moss over the stems to cover them completely, then wrap the string securely around them.

4 Bind on a couple of the darker peonies, their heads facing away from the single peony. Hide the stems under carpet moss, then tie off the string. Repeat along the rope, adding a few white "Duchesse de Nemours" peonies.

Opposite: Choose china to complement your color scheme. Here, the pale blue plates match the blue vases and intensify the cerise peonies.
Overleaf: Spacing the flowers for the garland at intervals along the rope will reduce your budget and allow you to splurge on a few more expensive flowers.

Posies

The bride's and bridesmaid's flowers reflect the relaxed, informal design of the table decorations. For the bride, I chose an all-white color scheme, based around white peonies, to stand out from the other flowers and marry with the peonies on the tables. I interspersed them with pure white roses (*Rosa*) and the pearl-like flowers of lily-of-the-valley (*Convallaria majalis*) to create a highly scented and romantic bouquet. I kept the bouquet small – about 8 inches in diameter because the lily-of-the-valley are so delicate – massing the flowers into a domed shape (see page 47) before tying them with a silvery-green ribbon.

The bridesmaid's flowers link all the flower elements together. Choosing the same basic garden flowers as for the table decorations, but incorporating several ivory varieties to match the bride's dress, I've managed to create an English-rose look that's in perfect harmony with its garden setting. The posy is created from blue forget-me-nots (*Myosotis*), pink cherry blossom (*Prunus*), pink-and-cerise peonies (*Paeonia*), the side shoots of blue delphiniums (*Delphinium*), green lady's mantle (*Alchemilla mollis*), and a mixture of burgundy, cream, and pink roses. For her hair, I made a circlet of the same flowers. This is something that needs practice and, especially when it's being made for a special occasion, is best left to someone with the relevant experience.

Opposite: When choosing flowers for a white or cream bouquet, it can be difficult to match the shades exactly with the bride's dress. To avoid any clashes, choose colors that contrast strongly and deliberately.

Above: The large, heady roses give the bridesmaid a nostalgic look.

Overleaf (clockwise from top left): examining the table; astilbe; an unexpected guest; delphiniums; peonies; grapes; strawberries; delphiniums.

Roses and berries

Opposite: To make the roses look as natural as possible, place the fuller flowers toward the center of the arrangement and position the smaller blooms, and the buds, around the edge, where they'll be most visible.

One of the great pleasures of using roses (*Rosa*) in arrangements is the fresh quality of their flowers and the delicacy of their petals. In a display like this, where several different varieties are massed together in a pitcher, the roses look at their very best. They've virtually been allowed to arrange themselves naturally, with the softer-stemmed varieties trailing lazily over the edge of the pitcher to give the arrangement a relaxed, informal feel.

Although these look like garden roses, they were in fact all grown commercially – the cream, open roses are "Champagne," the sugar pink ones are called "Blue Moon," the pale apricot ones are "Valerie," and the very dark red spray variety is "Red Ace." Part of the charm of the arrangement lies in the different stages of the roses, with some still in tight bud, some gradually unfurling their petals and others in full bloom.

"Champagne" is one of the very few commercially grown roses that open quickly like garden roses to show their stamens. Most varieties keep their shape until they become overblown, which can look rather formal. However, if you want your roses to open fully but you don't have the right varieties, you can doctor them to look like garden roses. This technique is especially valuable at those times of the year when garden roses aren't in season. Choose commercially grown roses with full heads, and gently pull out the central petals with your fingertips to reveal the golden stamens. You'll be left with roses that look as if they have been grown in your garden.

Choosing roses at differing stages of growth, as here, is another way of making them look as if they've just been picked from the garden, and of giving the arrangement an air of spontaneity. And mixing colors, or shades of a particular color, will enhance this look. A bouquet made up of just one variety of pink roses all in bud, for instance, will always look as if it has come straight from a florist.

For the container, I chose a straight-edged, sea-blue pitcher to contrast with the delicate, fluted rose petals. This is set off by two little bowls of jewel-like summer fruits that enhance the ruby-reds of the magenta roses and form a pool of color on the table beneath.

Candlelit dinner

Candles always add a sense of occasion when you dine outdoors, whether you have individual lanterns hanging on the walls, or groups of candlesticks on the table and, if the flowers are scented, the warmth of the candles will help to release their fragrance.

I made this candlestick by placing a thick candle in a terra-cotta flowerpot which I first wrapped in globe artichoke leaves (*Cynara scolymus*). I chose them for their attractive deep green color and interesting shape. If these leaves aren't available, you could use Savoy cabbage leaves (*Brassica oleracea bullata*), hosta (*Hosta*), bergenia (*Bergenia*), or large variegated ivy (*Hedera*) leaves.

The simple green and white color scheme is particularly effective in this informal yet stylish setting. If you are making the arrangement for your own garden, choose colors that are reflected in neighboring flowers and shrubs. This pot of white hydrangeas (*Hydrangea macrophylla*), lime-green Queen Anne's lace (*Daucus carota*), and white roses (*Rosa*) would also look good against a backdrop of standard marguerites, whose bushy form echoes the rounded shape of the hydrangeas. If your color scheme is pink, you could substitute pink hydrangeas for the white ones.

This small arrangement is ideal for an informal supper party, but you could make one on a grander scale using several candles.

1 You'll need two gladioli leaves (*Gladiolus*), several large globe artichoke leaves, a terra-cotta flowerpot, a sharp knife, a metal or plastic container to fit inside the pot, sphagnum moss, a large candle, and your flowers (see opposite). Start by conditioning the flowers by trimming at least an inch from their stems and leaving them to drink in cool water and flower-food for several hours. Tie the pointed ends of the gladioli leaves together to form a loose knot. Next, place the most attractive globe artichoke leaf on one side of the flowerpot, and center the gladioli knot over the leaf's central rib.

2 Arrange more globe artichoke leaves around the outside of the pot, then fasten them in place by knotting the gladioli leaves together at the back of the pot. If this is difficult, you could pin them together instead.

3 Using a sharp kitchen knife, trim the globe artichoke leaves flush with the base of the flowerpot.

4 Stand the pot upright on a flat surface. Place the metal or plastic container inside, and fill the cavity between the two pots with small pieces of sphagnum moss. Continue to add the moss until the container sits snugly inside, its rim completely level with that of the flowerpot. Arrange small fronds of moss neatly around the top.

5 Place the candle in the inner container and fill this with water to which you have added some flower-food.

6 Cut the flower heads short and arrange them in the inner container. Position the hydrangea heads between the globe artichoke leaves and intersperse them with the rose heads and sprigs of Queen Anne's lace.

Seed pack pot

Opposite: A vividly colored arrangement like this brightens up a shady table in the garden.
Overleaf (clockwise from top left): delphinium; ranunculus; September flower; pink sweet pea; violet pansy; orange ranunculus; pink ranunculus; cerise stock.

Wrapping empty seed packs around a terra-cotta pot and tying them with raffia is a colorful variation on the idea of wrapping plant leaves around a pot (see pages 142–3). All too often, seed packs get tucked away in drawers or thrown away, but I think their brightly colored photographs or Fifties-style illustrations are worth displaying, and provide an easy way of decorating a plain container.

For this arrangement, I chose loud, brightly colored seed packs to set off the rich, purple-velvet lisianthus (*Eustoma grandiflorum*), which I've cut short to accentuate their color and create a simple, compact shape. The packs are tied to the container with purple raffia and, once set against a backdrop of shocking pink tissue paper, create a riot of clashing colors. The result is a fun and quirky arrangement.

You can use any garden flowers for this style of arrangement, although the more cheerful their colors the more dramatic the look. There are many garden flowers that would look good, and which are easy to grow from seed; among them are orange, red, and yellow nasturtiums (*Tropaeolum majus*), orange and yellow pot marigolds (*Calendula officinalis*), purple, pink, and yellow pansies (*Viola x wittrockiana*), pink, purple, and red China asters (*Callistephus chinensis*), pink and orange godetias (*Godetia*), or pink, purple, and red sweet peas (*Lathyrus odoratus*).

This seed pack pot would make a marvelous gift, although it would be impractical to transport the cut flowers, in their water, very far. A safer bet might be to use a pot-grown plant in place of the cut flowers – a pelargonium (*Pelargonium*) would be ideal in the summer, or you could choose an indoor ornamental calamondin orange tree (*Citrus mitis*) in the winter. If flowers aren't your style, use pot-grown vegetables or herbs instead – a green and purple ornamental cabbage (*Brassica oleracea*) would look stunning in a pot wrapped in vegetable seed packs, as would an exotic lettuce, such as oakleaf or lollo biondo. As for herbs, there's a vast array to choose from, so select something that will appeal to the person who'll be receiving the gift.

Party time

I always try to encourage my children to appreciate and learn about flowers, as my father did with me and my sister when we were young. Simply making sure that there are always fresh flowers in the house is perhaps the best way of encouraging them, but here I've created an arrangement especially for them and their playhouse.

If you choose bright colors and simple shapes, you're bound to capture their imagination, so here I've used yellow marigolds (*Calendula officinalis*), pink China asters (*Callistephus chinensis*), and yellow goldenrod (*Solidago*), all of which can be grown easily from seed. Alternatives might include anemones (*Anemone*), ranunculus (*Ranunculus*), or gerbera (*Gerbera*).

The arrangements are so easy to make, you can even involve the children. Simply cut the stems to the same length and place generous handfuls into a selection of multi-colored cups. The plastic cups not only contribute to the bold and happy color scheme, but also have the advantage of being extremely practical – a bonus when there are young children running around!

You can adapt this idea for a grown-ups' party by using little tumblers of flowers to match the glassware, plates, and napkins. Lining them up down the center of the table to create bold splashes of color or arranging them as place settings makes a novel feature for an informal supper party.

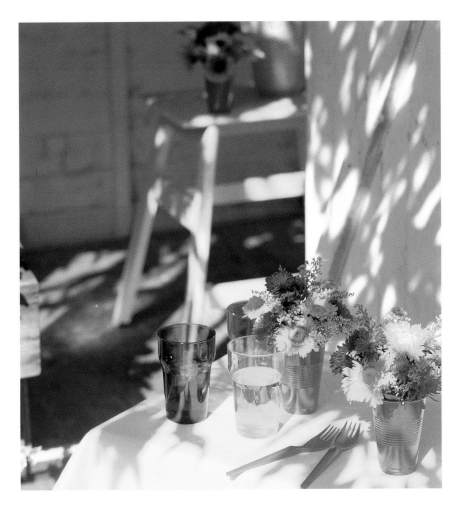

Opposite and above: These diminutive arrangements show that small is charming as well as beautiful. They would be extra special for a child if he or she had grown the flowers from seed.

Fruits and flowers

This elegant arrangement of tall, spiky "Blue Bees" delphiniums (*Delphinium belladonna*) and tumbling grapes would be perfect for an outdoor party on a balmy summer evening.

The combination of fruits and flowers in an arrangement has a timeless quality which was particularly celebrated in paintings by Dutch Old Masters. Here the arrangement is made sumptuous by trailing grapes and succulent fruits. The midnight-blues and iridescent greens are particularly effective for an evening celebration as they are enhanced by the candlelit setting. For an exotic display, combine glory lilies (*Gloriosa superba*) or "Minerva" amaryllis (*Hippeastrum*) with apricots, nectarines, cherries, and trails of berry fruits. Encourage your guests to help themselves!

In this table centerpiece, I used purple plums, navy blueberries, vivid limes, and green grapes, combining them with delphiniums and the trailing catkins of green love-lies-bleeding (*Amaranthus caudatus* "Viridis"). The contemporary wirework fruit bowl is particularly

effective in this display because it enables you to see most of the fruits.

1 To make the arrangement, you'll need a suitable fruit bowl, several small glass tumblers, which will be hidden inside the bowl, and the fruits and flowers. Place the tumblers in the middle of the fruit bowl, lodging them in position by placing the limes around the outside. Fill the tumblers with water.

2 Add the fruits, arranging them in piles to form blocks of different colors and textures. Drape the grapes over the edge of the fruit bowl, if necessary anchoring the main stalk with a few carefully placed limes or plums. Now arrange the flowers. Cut the delphiniums very short, so none of the stems will be visible, but still tall enough to add height, and place them right in the center. Finally, add the love-lies-bleeding, draping it elegantly over the side of the bowl so that it trails onto the table top. When adding flowers to edibles, make sure the flowers have not been sprayed and are edible varieties.

Opposite: You don't need armfuls of flowers to create an eye-catching centerpiece. Here, a small bunch of delphiniums and a single stem of love-lies-bleeding are arranged among a bowl of succulent fruits to create a decadent display of opulence.

CARE AND CONDITIONING

If you want arrangements to look their best, it's important to condition your flowers properly before you arrange them. Spending a few minutes looking after them before you put them in water can prolong their lifespan, sometimes by several days, and will enhance the attractiveness of the display.

CHOOSING YOUR FLOWERS

When you buy flowers, look at them carefully to ensure they are in good condition. Discard any bunches with slimy or flaccid leaves, damaged or floppy flower heads, or crushed stems. Consider how long the flowers have been in the store, because that will give you some idea of how fresh they are – if you're buying from a supermarket, it's easy, as the label will give you the sell-by date. Flowers that are being sold at a reduced price, because they're nearing their sell-by date, may not be the bargain that they first seem because they may fade in a couple of days. This won't matter if you're going to use the flowers almost immediately – say, for a special celebration – but it will be important if you want them to last for several days or more.

If you're buying flowers for a special occasion, you'll want them to look their very best, in which case you may prefer to buy them already in flower. If you want the flowers to last for as long as possible, however, you should choose them when they're still in bud, with the color of their petals just breaking through. Some flowers, such as peonies (*Paeonia*), poppies (*Papaver*), roses (*Rosa*), and irises (*Iris*), should not be bought in tight green bud because they will never open. The length of time that the buds take to open depends on the flower and also the air temperature – generally, the colder the temperature the more slowly the flowers will develop.

CONDITIONING THE FLOWERS

Although florists and market traders usually display their flowers in buckets or vases of water, the flowers will be out of water on your journey home. As a result, their stems will begin to dry out and, in the case of particularly susceptible flowers such as roses and gerbera (*Gerbera*), they may develop air-locks in their stems that can make their heads droop. So it's essential that you condition the flowers as soon as possible.

First of all, prepare the water in which you are going to condition the flowers. For this, you'll need a completely clean bucket or tall vase, which should be filled with cool water into which you have dissolved a packet of flower-food. Always use this, not only when conditioning the flowers but also in the finished arrangements, because it will help to prolong the life of the flowers and will also keep the water clean.

Now unwrap the flowers and remove any constricting rubber bands or twine holding the stems together. Strip off any leaves that are damaged or which will sit below the water line in your arrangement, as they will turn slimy if left on the stems. Remove any broken stems and use these flowers in tiny displays. With a sharp knife or pair of scissors, cut at least one inch from the bottom of each stem at a sharp angle. It is vital to do this because it not only removes any cell tissue that may have already dried out, but also enables the maximum surface area of the stem to take up water. As you cut each stem, immediately place it in the bucket or vase of conditioning water to prevent any air bubbles from forming. When you have prepared all the flowers in this way, leave them in the conditioning water, in a cool place, for at least two hours or overnight, if possible.

Some flowers have very pliable stems that will harden into contorted or peculiar positions if they aren't supported while being conditioned. Gerbera are particularly susceptible to this problem. To prevent it from happening, wrap the whole stems in newspaper before conditioning them. Make sure the stems are completely straight, with no kinks or bends, otherwise they'll still be there when the flowers are ready to be arranged. If you don't want the stems of tulips (*Tulipa*) to bend toward the light, do likewise and this will encourage them to stay straight.

Up until a few years ago, the traditional way to condition flowers and shrubs with woody stems was to hit them hard with a hammer, or to split them open with a knife. It was believed that this helped them to drink. Roses, lilac (*Syringa*), yarrow (*Achillea*), chrysanthemums (*Chrysanthemum*), heathers (*Erica, Calluna,* and *Daboecia*), forsythia (*Forsythia*), ivy (*Hedera*), and rosemary (*Rosmarinus*) were all said to benefit from this treatment. Now, however, it is thought that crushing a plant stem does more harm than good, because it makes the plant more susceptible to microbial attack (which can quickly kill it and may also damage the cells that take up water). So leave your hammer where it belongs in your tool chest and, instead, cut the stems at as sharp an angle as possible to expose the greatest possible surface area to the water. Stripping off

unwanted foliage or small branches will also help to prolong the life of woody-stemmed flowers and plants, because more water will be directed to the flowers instead of being wasted on the leaves.

FIRST AID FOR FLOWERS

When you get your flowers home, you may occasionally find that the stems are rather weak; this is particularly common with tulips and roses. A good way of strengthening them is to trim the stems as I've already described and then wrap them in sheets of newspaper before placing them in the conditioning water.

Some flowers are particularly vulnerable to bacterial attack, which will rapidly kill them. The best way to prevent this is to ensure that all the vases and containers are scrupulously clean. Whenever you empty them, tip out all the flower water and then scrub them in hot soapy water. When you rinse out the vases and containers, add a drop of bleach to the water to kill off any remaining bacteria and fungi.

If the flower heads start to droop while they're in the vase, you may be able to revive them but you'll have to act fast. Roses, gerbera, and sunflowers (*Helianthus*) are particularly prone to developing air-locks in their stems, which prevent them from taking up water. To revive them, remove them from the vase, trim at least one inch from the bottom of the stems, and wrap the whole stems in newspaper. Now place them up to their necks in a bucket of cool water and flower-food, and leave them overnight.

SPECIAL TREATMENTS

The vast majority of flowers need only simple conditioning to look their best. The following flowers, however, need special treatment.

Amaryllis (*Hippeastrum*)

These flowers have hollow stems which may need supporting, especially if used in tall arrangements. The traditional method is to turn the flower upside-down, fill the stem with water, and then plug it with a little piece of absorbent cotton. This is a good way to drench both yourself – and the floor – with water. It is much easier to push a thin bamboo cane inside the stem before conditioning the flowers. You won't even need to do this if you cut the stems very short. Amaryllis stems tend to split after a long time in water, but this can be remedied if you trim them occasionally.

Chinese lanterns (*Physalis*)

If left on the stems, the foliage of Chinese lanterns will quickly wilt and look unattractive, so as a preventative measure, always strip all the leaves from the stems before arranging the flowers.

Daffodils (*Narcissus*)

If you've ever picked daffodils from a garden, you'll know that they're full of a sticky sap. This may harm other flowers if you mix them together in a vase, and the other blooms may fade early. It isn't usually a problem if you use only a few daffodils in a mixed arrangement, but if you need more than this you should condition them separately for 24 hours before combining them with the other flowers. Alternatively, you can buy a special flower-food for mixed arrangements that prevents the sap from damaging the other flowers.

Delphiniums (*Delphinium*)

Some large flowers, such as delphiniums, may have rather weak stems that need extra support. The traditional method is to fill the stems with water, in the same way as for amaryllis, but this is very time-consuming. I prefer to insert thin canes into the stems. To prolong the life of the flowers, strip off any lower leaves so that all the water is directed toward the flower heads.

Euphorbia (*Euphorbia*)

Take care when handling euphorbia stems because their sap can cause painful skin irritations. Stop the sap from leaching out and weakening other flowers in the vase by singeing the cut stem with a lighted match or candle. After a few days in water, the foliage of *Euphorbia fulgens* will turn yellow, but you can carefully remove it, leaving just the flowers.

Hellebores (*Helleborus*)

To prevent these flowers drooping, seal the milky sap inside their stems by searing the ends with a lighted candle or match.

Lilies (*Lilium*)

Lilies have long and attractive stamens which will stain anything that comes into contact with them. They can shed pollen onto the flower petals, which sometimes looks unsightly, and they can also drop this pollen onto tablecloths and tabletops. The pollen can stain your skin and also your clothes (which is particularly disastrous at weddings), so as a preventive measure, always remove the stamens when you condition lilies. If the worst does happen and your clothes become stained with lily pollen, remove it by picking it off with a piece of cellophane tape. Resist the temptation to rub at it, because this will smear the dye into the fabric.

Poppies (*Papaver*)

Poppies picked from gardens don't last long in water and soon drop their petals, but commercially grown varieties can last for several days. Their stems contain a lot of sap which quickly leaches out and makes the flowers droop. To seal them, trim the poppy stems to the right length for your arrangement, then singe the end of each one

with a lighted match or candle. When the petals eventually fall, the remaining seed heads look most attractive, and can either stay in the arrangement or be used again in another one.

Sunflowers (*Helianthus*)

If the petals start to look untidy, carefully pull them out with your fingers. You'll be left with the central seeds surrounded by the small green calyx, which looks very striking and attractive.

Zinnias (*Zinnia*)

The stems of these brightly colored summer flowers can quickly deteriorate, but you can delay this process by using flower-food and changing the water every day.

POISONOUS PLANTS

Some plants and flowers are poisonous, or contain sap that can irritate your skin and cause rashes, burns, or blisters. Handle them with care – touch them as little as possible and keep them away from children. Poisonous plants include arum lilies (*Arum italicum*), euphorbias (*Euphorbia*), foxgloves (*Digitalis purpurea*), glory lilies (*Gloriosa superba*), hellebores (*Helleborus*), ivy (*Hedera*), laburnum (*Laburnum anagyroides*), lily-of-the-valley (*Convallaria majalis*), monkshood (*Aconitum napellus*), rue (*Ruta graveolens*), and yew (*Taxus baccata*). Plants containing sap that can cause skin irritations include arum lilies, euphorbias, ivy, primula (*Primula obconica*), and rue, which should never be handled in bright sunlight because this can trigger a severe skin reaction and cause blistering.

If you suspect poisoning from a plant, consult your doctor or local hospital immediately, taking a piece of the plant with you and the plant label, if you have it. Don't try to make the affected person vomit, as this may be harmful. If the skin or eyes are irritated by a plant, wash the area with clean water and, if necessary, seek medical help. Again, take a piece of the plant and its label with you.

Page 154: Gerbera, roses, hyacinth, and eucalyptus
Opposite (clockwise from top left): foxglove, Christmas rose, widow iris, sweet pea

INDEX

A

air-locks 46, 155

amaryllis (*Hippeastrum*) 45, 155

anenomes 19, 82, 85

artichokes 128, 142–3

arum lilies (*Zantedeschia aethiopica*) 24

B

bacterial attack 155

baskets

wicker 27, 68

wire 16, 113, 150–1

bathroom arrangements 107, 115

bedroom arrangements 66, 80, 96–7

berries 20, 25, 62

blue flowers 105, 114

bouquet, bridal 46–9, 136–7

C

cabbage, ornamental

(*Brassica oleracea*) 128

candles 50, 128, 142–3

children 149

chillies 14, 20

Chinese lanterns (*Physalis*) 27, 155

Chinese meal 27

choosing, flowers 154

Christmas 20–3, 45, 50, 72

city-style arrangements 8–53

conditioning 46–7, 154–6

containers

baskets 16, 27, 68, 113, 150–1

china 61

city-style 11–13

complementary 81, 94–5

country style 54–9

hanging 44–5, 106–8

outdoor arrangements 122–5

porous 19

sea-style arrangements 103, 106–13

small 66, 96

test tubes 40–1, 45

vases 24, 106–8

wrapped 36, 142–5

country-style arrangements 54–97

D

daffodils 63, 156

dates, ornamental 36

delphiniums 150–1, 156

dinner parties 14, 27, 32–3, 128, 142–3

dried flowers 53, 68–77, 105

driftwood 113

E

euphorbia 156

F

feathers 114

foliage 20, 26, 40, 62

fragrance

flowers 24, 86

foliage 20, 40, 62

scented oils 72, 114

freshness 154

frosting 50

fruit 42–3, 50, 140–1, 150–1

G

garden-style arrangements 79

garlands 20–3, 132–5

gerbera 14–16, 31, 82

glass

colored 38–9

jars 110, 114

test tubes 40–1, 45

vases 24, 106–8

globe artichokes (*Cynara scolymus*) 128, 142–3

green flowers 26

H

Halloween 30–3

hallway arrangements 94–5

hellebores 156

herbaceous border flowers 79

herbs 126–7

I

irises 154

K

kitchen arrangement 65

L

lavender 73

lilies 24, 156

long-lasting flowers 24, 26, 36, 81, 95, 113

long-lasting foliage 20, 26, 40

M

mantelpiece arrangement 50–1

minimalism 19, 72

moss 40, 43, 76, 113

Mother's Day 19

N

narcissus 18–19

nostalgic arrangements 80

O

orchid (*Phalaenopsis*) 112–13

outdoor arrangements 120–57

P

patio, sea-style arrangement 114

pebbles 105–7, 110, 114

peonies 132, 154

poisonous plants 156

poppies (*Papaver*) 154, 156

posies 34–5, 47, 82, 137

potpourri 68, 114

protea 36–7

pumpkins 25, 30–3

purple flowers 95

R

ranunculus 81–2, 92–3

red flowers 53, 82

reviving flowers 155

rope 105, 110

roses

    arrangements 66, 80, 140–1

    care 46–7, 154

    dried 52–3, 72

    posies and bouquets 34–5, 46–9

    Valentine's Day 52–3

S

salal leaf wreath 40–1

sand 110

sea holly (*Eryngium*) 105

sea-style arrangements 98–119

seed pods 14, 25

shells 105–7, 110, 114

skin irritations 156

speedwell (*Veronica*) 105

spring flowers 61

stems

    care 27, 46, 155

    shortened 66, 86

    wreath base 40

stocks 96

summer flowers 131

sunflowers (*Helianthus*) 129, 156

T

table arrangements 32–3, 42, 61, 126–7, 149

terra-cotta pots 59, 68, 124, 128, 143

test tubes 40–1, 45

topiary trees 18–19, 53, 74–7

trachelium 110

tulips 14–16, 27, 45, 86–9

V

Valentine's Day 52–3

vases 24, 106–8

vegetables 14, 42–3, 128, 142–3

W

weddings 46–9, 131–7

white flowers 114

wicker baskets 27, 56, 68

wrapping

    containers 142–5

    posies and bouquets 34–5, 47

wreaths 40–3, 56

Z

zinnias 156

PUBLISHER'S ACKNOWLEDGMENTS

The publisher would like to thank the following for providing locations for photography: **Jennifer Alexander**; Jackie Altfield at **Holt Antique Centre**, Holt, Norfolk 01263 712097; **Brocante**, Rectory Grove, Leigh-on-Sea, Essex, 01702 470756; **Helen Fickling**; **Nick Grossmark** and **Graeme Merton**; **Fianne Stanford** at Kirker Greer, Belvedere Road, Burnham-on-Crouch, Essex, 01621 784647; **Karen McDonald Thomas**, 2, Chapel Yard, Holt, Norfolk, 01263 713935; **Christine Stafferton**; and **Wright and Teague**, and **Tudor Rose** (0181 288 0999) for supplying dried flowers.

The publisher would also like to thank **Carolyn Harris** and **Elspeth Alexander** for appearing in the book and **Isabel de Cordova**, **Amanda Lerwill** and **Kirsty O'Leary Leeson** for their help in producing it.

AUTHOR'S ACKNOWLEDGMENTS

I have loved every moment of producing this book – from start to finish it has been heaven! To work with a team like this doesn't happen often, and I'd like to thank and praise them all enormously, as without each individual playing his or her role and contributing so much it could never have happened. *My thanks:*

Firstly to Simon Brown, who captured everything on film in a way I had only dreamed of and produced breathtaking photographs; to Leslie Harrington, who art directed the book, for her careful selection of photographs from thousands, and for the combinations and layouts she produced which are absolutely stunning. I can't thank her enough for her patience and eye for perfection; to Jane Struthers, who sat tirelessly through my wondering about the beauty of individual flowers and put it into the written word; to Cathy Sinker, who searched everywhere for the perfect vase or cloth in just the right color and always found it; and to Jenna Jarman, for nagging, pushing, pulling us all nicely into shape until we achieved as near perfection as possible – and what's more, we did it on time! – seriously, thank you.

To all my team at the shops and school – without them, projects like this just would not be possible. They allowed me to escape while they carried on running everything like clockwork. Thank you to everyone behind the scenes who pulled everything together and made it all work, and finally to Gary, because without him this definitely wouldn't have happened.